A Search for Competitive Advantage

This shortform book presents key peer-reviewed research selected by expert series editors and contextualised by new analysis from each author on how British industrial firms achieved a competitive advantage.

With contributions on industrial cartelisation, organisational structure, the quality of British management, marketing and trade marks, labour relations, and technological innovation, this volume provides an array of fascinating insights into industrial history.

Of interest to business and economic historians, this shortform book also provides analysis and illustrative case-studies that will be valuable reading across the social sciences.

John F. Wilson is Pro Vice-Chancellor (Business and Law) at Northumbria University at Newcastle.

Steven Toms spent fifteen years in senior management at Nottingham University as head of the undergraduate programme, chair of teaching committee and research director before becoming Head of York Management School in 2004.

Ian Jones is a Senior Research Assistant at Newcastle Business School, Northumbria University.

Routledge Focus on Industrial History
Series Editors: John F. Wilson, Steven Toms and Ian Jones

This Shortform series presents key peer-reviewed research originally published in the *Journal of Industrial History*, selected by expert series editors and contextualised by new analysis from each author on how the specific field addressed has evolved.

Of interest to business historians, economic historians and social scientists interested in the development of key industries, the series makes theoretical and conceptual contributions to the field, as well as providing a plethora of empirical, illustrative and detailed case-studies of industrial developments in Britain, the United States and other international settings.

For more information about this series, please visit: www.routledge.com/
Routledge-Focus-on-Industrial-History/book-series/RFIH

A Search for Competitive Advantage

Case Studies in Industrial History

Edited by John F. Wilson, Steven Toms, and Ian Jones

Routledge
Taylor & Francis Group

LONDON AND NEW YORK

First published 2021
by Routledge
2 Park Square, Milton Park, Abingdon, Oxon OX14 4RN

and by Routledge
605 Third Avenue, New York, NY 10158

Routledge is an imprint of the Taylor & Francis Group, an informa business

British Library Cataloguing-in-Publication Data
A catalogue record for this book is available from the British Library

Library of Congress Cataloging-in-Publication Data
Names: Wilson, John, editor. | Jones, Ian (Senior research assistant)
    editor. | Toms, Steven, editor.
Title: A search for competitive advantage : case studies in industrial
    history / edited by John Wilson, Ian Jones and Steven Toms.
Description: New York : Routledge, 2021. | Series: Routledge
    focus on industrial history | Includes bibliographical references
    and index.
Identifiers: LCCN 2021007631 (print) | LCCN 2021007632
    (ebook)
Subjects: LCSH: Industries—Great Britain—History. | Branding
    (Marketing)—Great Britain—History. | Trademarks—
    Great Britain—History. | Organizational change—Great
    Britain—History.
Classification: LCC HC253 .S43 2021 (print) | LCC HC253
    (ebook) | DDC 338.0941—dc23
LC record available at https://lccn.loc.gov/2021007631
LC ebook record available at https://lccn.loc.gov/2021007632

ISBN: 978-0-367-02415-4 (hbk)
ISBN: 978-1-032-05459-9 (pbk)
ISBN: 978-0-429-39973-2 (ebk)

Typeset in Times New Roman
by Apex CoVantage, LLC

Contents

Tables

Contributors

Roy Church was formerly Emeritus Professor at the University of East Anglia and was President of the Association of Business Historians from 1995 to 1996. He has published extensively on the history of advertising and marketing in Britain and the British car industry.

David Higgins completed his PhD in economics at the University of Cambridge. He has worked as a Lecturer/Senior Lecturer in economics at the University of Sheffield, held a Personal Chair in Business History and Managerial Economics at the University of York, and is currently a Professor in the Accounting and Financing Division at Newcastle University Business School. He has published numerous papers on the British cotton textile industry, and the development and protection of geographical indications, merchandise marks, and trade marks. He has written and edited four books, the most recent of which being *Brands, Geographical Origin, and the Global Economy: A History from the Nineteenth Century to the Present* (CUP, 2018).

Peter King completed his PhD at the University of Wolverhampton on the iron trade in England and Wales between 1500 and 1815. Both before and after that, he has published extensively on the iron industry, local history, the history of transport, and has recently published a two-volume book titled *A Gazetteer of the British Iron Industry, 1490–1815*. He is currently an Honorary Research Fellow at the University of Birmingham.

Introduction

Purpose and significance of the series

The concept of the *Routledge Focus on Industrial History* series was motivated by the desire of the editors to provide an outlet for articles originally published in the defunct *Journal of Industrial History* (*JIH*). By using an extensive repository of top-quality publications, the series will ensure that the authors' findings contribute to recent debates in the field of management and industrial history. Indeed, the articles contained in these volumes will appeal to a wide audience, including business historians, economic historians, and social scientists interested in longitudinal studies of the development of key industries and themes. Moreover, the series will provide fresh insight into how the academic field has developed over the past 20 years.

The editors believe that the quality of scholarship evident in the articles originally published in the *JIH* now deserve a much broader audience. The peer-reviewed articles are built on robust business-historical research methodologies and are subject to extensive primary research. The series will make important theoretical and conceptual contributions to the field and provide a plethora of empirical, illustrative, and detailed case studies of industrial developments in the United Kingdom, the United States, and other international settings. The collection will be of interest to a broad stratum of social scientists, especially business school and history department academics, because it provides valuable material that can be used in both teaching and research.

Building on the original *Journal of Industrial History*

The first edition of the *Journal of Industrial History* was published in 1998, with the aim of providing 'clear definitional parameters for industrial historians' and in turn establishing links between 'industrial history and theoretical work in social science disciplines like economics, management (including international business), political science, sociology, and anthropology'. Because it has been more than 20 years since its original publication, it is clear that the relevance of the *JIH* has stood the test of time. The original *JIH* volumes covered a diverse range of topics, including industrial structure and behaviour, especially in manufacturing and services; industrial and business case studies; business strategy and structure; nationalisation and privatisation; globalisation and competitive advantage; business culture and industrial development; education, training and human resources; industrial relations and its institutions; the relationship between financial institutions and industry; industrial politics, including the formulation and impact of industrial and commercial policy; and industry and technology. The current *Routledge Focus on Industrial History* series will provide a cross-section of articles that cover a wide range themes and topics, many of which remain central to management studies. These include separate volumes: *Management and Industry*; *Banking and Finance*; and *Growth and Decline of American Industry*. Future volumes in the series will cover case studies in knowledge managment; the development of professional management; and the cotton and textile industry. The *Routledge Focus on Industrial History* series will reframe highly original material that illustrates a wide variety of themes in management and organisation studies, including entrepreneurship, strategy, family business, trust, networks, and international business, focusing on topics such as the growth of the firm, crisis management, governance, management, and leadership.

Volume six: contribution and key findings

The sixth volume of this series focuses on sources of competitive advantage in industrial history. This volume examines sources of competitive advantage that organisations have harnessed ranging in date from the seventeenth century to the twentieth century and focusing on British based organisations. However, whilst these articles focus on British based organisations and industries, they are international in scope, showing how these businesses' search for competitive advantage included expanding into foreign markets and capturing external resources.

The first chapter, 'The origins of competitive advantage in the marketing of branded packaged consumer goods: Colman's and Reckitt's in early Victorian Britain', is a study by Roy Church and Christine Clark that analyses the development of the marketing strategies of two small to medium-sized family businesses during the nineteenth century. This chapter shows that modern marketing practices, such as employing salesmen, branding products, or systematic advertising, were not only practices by large businesses, but could also be used by small to medium-sized businesses as they attempted to grow to become large businesses. This chapter also shows that these marketing strategies were part of a planned strategy that linked product development, branding, advertising, and selling to create customer demand for their products, thereby encouraging more shops to stock them. Church and Clark show that by linking product development to branding, advertising, and selling, Reckett's and Colman's were able to apply the same techniques to their ranges of products with few problems.

The second chapter, 'The cartel in oregrounds iron: trading relationships in the raw material for steel' by Peter King, discusses the British iron and steel industry between the seventeenth and nineteenth centuries. This chapter shows how British iron and steel producers attempted to control supplies of Swedish oregrounds iron, coveted for its superior quality and necessary for the production of high-quality steel. King's work shows how early Sheffield steelmakers were likely responsible for the origins of a cartel, purchasing and closing rival steel furnaces to maintain control over steel production and influencing much of the oregrounds iron imports as they were the main purchasers. However, this chapter also shows how the cartel changed over time as the producers and importers of oregrounds iron, rather than iron and steel producers in Sheffield, began to exercise control. By limiting the production of oregrounds iron and controlling the distribution by insisting that the iron was sold by the same merchant, producers were able to maintain a high price for their products. At the same time, the use of long-term contracts allowed those merchants to maintain control of the supply. This control over a necessary resource for high-quality steel production gave British steel producers a competitive advantage over foreign competitors, enabling them to produce high-quality steel products that could not be produced elsewhere.

The final chapter is an article by David M. Higgins titled 'Made in Britain'? National trade marks and merchandise marks: the British experience from the late nineteenth century to the 1920s'. This chapter shows one response of British manufacturers to German competition in the domestic market in the form of a campaign to establish a 'Made in the British Empire' trade mark to oppose the 'Made in Germany' trade mark, something that was seen as advantageous for German manufacturers. However, whilst such a trade mark may have conferred a competitive advantage on smaller manufacturers, more prominent firms with their own established marks opposed the scheme. Additionally, issues on which products would be allowed to use the mark, whether applying the mark would be mandatory, and who would be responsible for enforcing the correct use of the trade mark led to the plans being abandoned.

Conclusions

It is apparent from this brief review of the chapters that the sixth volume in the series makes important contributions to the field of industrial history in several ways. Firstly, it provides a series of high calibre and unique studies in aspects of industrial history that contribute to the more recent debates on competitive advantage, cartelisation of industries, and marketing and the use of trade marks. Secondly, the chapters shed light on the broader subjects of technological innovation, disruption, and international trade.

Finally, this volume provides strong historical case-studies that can be used by students and researchers who are exploring ideas on sources of competitive advantage in British industrial history. The editors believe that this volume will not only provide a much wider audience for articles that link into a range of topical issues but also feed into debates in the wider social sciences. These are themes that will be developed further in subsequent volumes of the *Routledge Series of Industrial History*, highlighting the intrinsic value in republishing material from the *Journal of Industrial History* and ensuring that the articles contribute extensively to current debates.

1 The origins of competitive advantage in the marketing of branded packaged consumer goods*

Colman's and Reckitt's in early Victorian Britain

Roy Church and Christine Clark

In his analysis of British 'personal capitalism', Chandler qualified his condemnation of British business by specifically exempting those family firms in which in the late nineteenth century 'entrepreneurs were most successful: in the production of branded, packaged products'.[1] He observed that by 1900, producers of branded goods were among the nation's largest and most successful enterprises, particularly in the markets for food, drink, tobacco, dry goods groceries, and consumer chemicals. Fitzgerald's history of *Rowntree and the Marketing Revolution* highlighted the period between 1875 and 1914 when 'advances in technology and greater throughputs had enabled firms to increase and cheapen production for a burgeoning consumer market . . . advertising became a prominent activity, the large scale production of consumer goods enabling key firms to support substantial advertising costs'.[2] He described the essential characteristics of marketing modernity. They consisted of product development, direct selling, branding, and advertising, all dominant features in the consumer goods sector during the late nineteenth century when 'the second industrial revolution created the circumstances, which necessitated marketing'.[3] Evidence of these from 1875 in the case of the soap makers, Pears,[4] from 1885 in W. H. Lever's enterprise,[5] together with Bovril in the 1870s, and Bryant & May in the 1880s,[6] has led those seeking to generalise the development of modern marketing to identify these as having been among the most important first movers.[7] Thus, perhaps mainly because of the lack of evidence for the earlier period, the literature conveys the impression that the origins of modern marketing are to be found during the late nineteenth century and associated with large scale production by big companies.[8] Their observations are valid to a point; they help to explain the growth in direct selling, branding, advertising, and product development during the late nineteenth century which Rowntree's history amply delineates for the trade in chocolate. The definition of modern marketing emerging from this literature is also helpful (though, like all definitions, potentially a hostage to fortune). There is as yet, however, no satisfactory substantively documented account and explanation of the character and *origins* of modern marketing which preceded the manifestations in the well-documented histories of the chocolate and soap trades.[9]

A marketing revolution?

It is clear from Nevett's history of advertising that some elements in modern marketing were not completely novel in late nineteenth century Britain.[10] He referred to Schweppe's mineral water which was advertised from the late eighteenth century, as was Day & Martin's blacking; Fry's chocolate was also being advertised in the eighteenth century.[11] Horniman's tea was advertised from 1826, followed by Crosse & Blackwell's pickles, Robinson's patent barley water, and Huntley & Palmer's biscuits.[12] Patent medicines were promoted by heavy expenditure on commercial advertising during the early nineteenth century.[13] Extravagant images and often lurid texts were placed in newspapers and magazines in attempts to engage the attention and interest of potential users. However, the significance of this visual evidence of advertising is ambiguous. Berridge has suggested that the contribution of patent medicine vendors to the history of advertising during this period was perverse, and that the typically excessive hyperbole which patent medicine vendors employed tended to undermine the credibility of advertising generally. This prompted some editors to ban their advertisements.[14]

As for the references to advertisements for food and household goods before the 1870s, with the exception of Schweppe and Fry[15] (who were continuous advertisers from the beginning of the nineteenth century),[16] there is insufficient detailed evidence to justify describing their marketing activities as modern in the sense defined above. Did their advertisements form part of a substantial and sustained marketing policy which included direct selling by travellers, rather than selling only through commission agents, and did the advertisers attempt more than merely to inform potential customers of the existence of products available? The histories of Fry and Huntley & Palmer suggest that such an inference from advertisements may not be justified. In 1866, the Frys spent £2000 on advertising. This represented barely 1 per cent of sales, rising to roughly 5 per cent after 1890. Throughout that time, selling was through commission agents.[17] Corley's account of the nineteenth century marketing activities of Huntley & Palmer (regarded as one of the 'first movers') also underlines the need for scepticism. He maintained that from its formation in 1822, for most of the nineteenth century, the partners relied on personal trial and recommendation to publicise their biscuits, supplemented by little more than 'occasional nudges in the press'.[18] However, unlike Fry, Huntley & Palmer did employ travellers. The first was appointed in 1849. Eight were employed by the early 1870s.[19] It was not, however, until the 1890s, under pressure of competition from Peek Frean, which also employed salesmen and which Corley described as a new 'pace-setter' in advertising, that a policy of sustained mass advertising was introduced. This was the period, he noted, when Huntley & Palmer's biscuits joined Pears' and Sunlight soaps from Lever, Horniman's and Mazzawattee teas, and Fry's and Cadbury's chocolate and cocoa, all of which were already household words.[20]

However, searching for the origins of modern marketing is bedevilled by a lack of empirical evidence derived from the late nineteenth and early twentieth centuries. Even so, historians have tended to attribute the emergence of marketing modernity to large firms which, in the late nineteenth century, were able to afford advertising expenditure.[21] Evidence is presented below which documents earlier origins and suggests that advertising was not simply a consequence of size of firm. Advertising may, indeed, have been a method by which a number of small to medium-sized firms became large. For example, Cadbury emerged from serious financial difficulty in the 1860s by introducing cocoa essence, a new product which was promoted by heavy and sustained advertising. By so doing, Cadbury challenged Fry's virtually monopolistic position in the trade.[22] The only available indications of the comparative size of the two firms are numbers employed: Cadbury employed 12 people in 1861, 230 by the end of the 1870s;[23] employees at Fry already numbered 193 in 1867 (one year after cocoa essence was launched).[24]

Generalisation is impossible, for whereas retailing has attracted historians' attention in recent years,[25] developments in marketing, from the standpoint of the producer, have not. This study explores the origins of modern marketing. It relies primarily on evidence from two small to medium-sized family enterprises, though both of the successor companies figured among the leading national companies by the end of the century.[26] While neither Reckitt nor Colman was the first to employ salesmen, brand products, or to advertise in a recognisably modern, sustained, and systematic method, both were certainly among the first British manufacturers of branded, packaged consumer goods to combine all of these. Well before the end of the century, Colman's mustard, starch, and washing blues and Reckitt's starches, washing blues, and blacking were household names, not only in Britain but increasingly, from the 1870s, in Continental Europe, North and South America, and throughout the British Empire. One outcome was that by the early 1900s, as a result of several decades during which marketing innovation was a vital factor contributing to the success of the two enterprises, both figured among Britain's largest 100 manufacturing companies which were also multinationals.[27] They may not have been the first, but the richness of the archives illuminates vividly the development of marketing methods during the period. Their history also throws light on the foundations of British marketing pre-eminence in the branded packaged consumer goods industry during the under-researched mid-nineteenth century. Hence their importance as contributors to the foundation of competitive advantage in what subsequently became one of Britain's leading industrial sectors.

'. . . a dazzling whiteness': product development at the firm of Isaac Reckitt

Once legislative reform had removed the legal and tax-related barriers to entry into the starch industry[28] intense competition developed. The technology of starch production during this period remained relatively simple. While steam was applied to the milling process, the transformation of wheat (and later rice) into starch was essentially achieved through repeated washing, pounding, filtration, sieving, and settling, interspersed with fresh water supplies pumped into and out of tank containers. Drying, pressing (later using hydraulics), and cutting in preparation for packing and shipment followed recovery of the starch through sedimentation and draining.[29] Initially purchased ready-made for re-sale to grocers, like starch, black lead was also produced by milling and mixing and did not require heavy capital investment. Technical economies of scale, therefore, were not significant. Consequently when the demand for starch expanded, new entrants removed the possibility that established manufacturers might sell without the effort needed to attract buyers.

Entrants set the pace partly by introducing price competition. However, these starch makers also employed strategies which included product differentiation by experimenting with new starches, introducing new products and new product lines, variations in packaging, targeted selling, and advertising. Each of these dimensions of competition which changed a long-established traditional industry, supplying starch primarily for luxury consumption to popular use, is examined below. Unlike soap, neither starch nor blue possessed a capacity to clean; none the less, the stiffening and whitening qualities of starch and the extra whitening effect of blue were in growing demand, one outcome of an increasing tendency among Victorians to associate cleanliness with respectability and both with whiteness. As a result, laundering using starch and blue was essential if clothing and linen were to conform to an enduring fashion. As an inexpensive item in absolute terms, especially after the deregulation of the trade in 1834, these ingredients soon became affordable luxuries in demand for widespread, though not necessarily frequent, consumption among all classes.[30]

Following a series of business ventures launched by Isaac Reckitt, each of which failed, the breakthrough which laid the foundations for success occurred in the mid-1840s. The starch enterprise had begun in 1840, at a time when deregulation of the industry offered opportunities for innovation.[31] Following a Select Committee inquiry which reported in 1834, the complicated, highly proscriptive system of regulation, inspection, and heavy taxation of starch was removed. This ended the dominance of the handful of large, patent-based London starch makers.[32] In 1836, Isaac's eldest son, Frederic Reckitt, then aged 21, showed an amateur interest in chemistry. At that time, quality control in the manufacture of starch was akin to cookery and favoured experimentation as a method of improving the product and maintaining standards. Frederic, the firm's only chemist for nearly fifty years, has been described as 'caring but little about the purely commercial side of the business'.[33] During most of that period, he alone conducted the experiments and tests required for the manufacture and improvement of Reckitt's products. In 1844, Isaac Reckitt is believed to have acquired a recipe for soluble starch made from sago in settlement of a debt.[34] At Isaac's request Frederic succeeded (by adding acid) in producing a crystalline starch which, unlike its predecessors, was soluble in hot water and which could be made either from farina or from the cheaper substitute, sago. Francis wrote to Frederic: 'I am still ignorant by what means thou used the magic rod to produce such envied results.'[35]

A financial liquidity crisis, which hit the business in 1847, led to a review of policy. The discovery that since 1844, soluble starch had been profitable, whereas traditional powder starch, which comprised the bulk of all sales, had not, led to an increased search for lines to replace powder starches. As competition increased, evidence of which was the frequency with which other starchmakers were visiting grocers,[36] the Reckitts concentrated attention on product development. The first result from more than 20 experiments George conducted in 1849 was that of dietetic arrow root. This was made from farina, sold through grocers, chemists, and druggists, and aimed at the health foods market; it was not, however, a success in competition with genuine arrow root.[37] More successful was the application of chlorate to produce a superior patent wheaten starch for domestic purposes and for use by Nottingham lace finishers. In terms normally associated with a much later era of modern advertising, he described this starch as possessing 'a more dazzling whiteness than anything yet produced'.[38] Capital was borrowed from Albert Reckitt, Isaac's nephew, to concentrate on the development of the new lines.[39] Whiteness was to feature in the advertising campaign planned to launch the new product[40] and explains why George suggested that blues, for whitening and colouring starches and potentially sold to paper makers, would be a valuable way of spreading travellers' costs.[41] Isaac had first used smalts (a natural but increasingly scarce blue pigment) when he had begun starch making for the purpose of countering yellowing.[42] At the same time, the supply of artificial ultramarine blue had increased since the 1840s, mainly by a growing number of producers mainly in Germany, and made further development of a trade in blue possible.[43] When blue, purchased for use but also for sale, began on a substantial scale in 1852 an important new product was added to the Reckitt range which from 1884 the company began to manufacture. George argued that, regardless of the direction which diversification might take, Reckitt's needed 'to be first so as not to be seen to be imitating'.[44]

Selling groceries: Colman's and Reckitt's on the road

Effective selling was necessary if Frederic's efforts to diversify product lines were to succeed. At first, Isaac had relied on wholesale and commission agents who, in some instances, combined their work for Reckitt's with that of other (usually Quaker) firms. The discounts on prices which agents received varied according to quality and volume; Isaac fixed the prices which retailers had to observe. However, beginning in 1850, George expressed reservations concerning the effectiveness of relying upon commission agents 'to win the retailers over' and urged the adoption of more direct selling.[45]

In both firms, family members were the first to go on the road. James Colman began at the age of 24 in 1825 and Edward Colman, aged 19, in 1827. By the 1850s, five travellers covered the country districts and two worked from the London office.[46] By 1874, the figure was eleven in the country and five in London.[47] On Isaac Reckitt's entry into the starch trade, he had relied on large merchant wholesalers as agents, notably Storey, Smithson & Newham. This arrangement during a cyclical downturn rendered the Reckitt enterprise vulnerable.[48] As the father of an adolescent family, Isaac faced a dilemma. He was reluctant to engage travellers from outside the family, partly because of cost, the risks of embezzlement, and the problem of exercising control. However, low or non-existent profitability produced increasingly serious cash flow problems as the economy faltered during the early 1840s. This forced reconsideration. Selling through agents on commission swallowed up the profits from trading, consequently it was in order to save costs and to reduce reliance on agents that in 1843, Isaac agreed to his eldest son George's request to go on the road at the age of 18. Two more Reckitt sons, Francis (aged 21) in 1848, and James (aged 17) in 1850 soon joined their brother.[49]

Isaac proved to be a hard taskmaster. During the late 1840s, a liquidity shortage prompted agents to press for heavy discounts on substantial orders.[50] The rapid settlement of accounts by purchasers became crucial to the survival of the family business. The failure of Storey, Smithson & Newham (who normally sold 5 cwt of Reckitt's starch weekly) to sell any at all for more than two months in 1847, meant that raw materials could not be purchased. This threatened production. The liquidity crisis underlined the importance of a continual, if relatively small, cash flow advanced by George's collection of debts on his travels.[51] 'Above all, bring in the money', was the injunction that brought one of Isaac's letters to a close.[52] Requesting that he stay longer in the field to collect, Isaac admonished George in 1847: 'Thou must not lightly leave accounts till next time . . . I should urge you rather strongly'; and again, 'It neutralises all my diligence's and anxiety in behalf of customers and ourselves.'[53] Economy and the imperative for debt collectors to be trustworthy meant that in the firm's formative years, travellers were confined to the family. As the business expanded and the pressure on the Reckitt sons intensified, attitudes changed. George Reckitt noted the frequency ('a dozen or more a month') with which grocers were called upon by competing starchmakers, the principal competitors (who were already advertising) being Brown & Poulson, Anderson, Glenfield, and Colman.[54] After seven days in Manchester, up at 5.30 am and working until 9 o'clock at night, he agonised: 'my legs would not take me anywhere else. I should not work so hard could I see a reasonable prospect of finishing these huge places without.'[55] Liverpool, Warrington, Chester, and other northern towns awaited him on this journey. From Liverpool, George explained how long it took to make all his calls and that furthermore 'until we get the advertising at work and push right and left with it, so as to create a demand, it will not do much good.'[56] Advertising was one element in the 'tactics more practical than the present', which George was convinced was the only way to supplant Brown & Poulson's dominance in the north of England market for starch.[57] He urged his father to give advertising a year's trial: 'see something of the way the wind blows, and if against us let us retire from it before all the banknotes are blown out of our cash box'.[58]

When in 1850, James joined brothers Francis and George on the road, he, too, experienced the rigours of open carriage third class rail travel and coaches.[59] The brothers' letters convey their frustration at what they perceived to be uncongenial environments and the unappealing characteristics of local inhabitants.[60] Worst of all, however, were not encounters with the general public but the company of other travellers. The Reckitts preferred to frequent Temperance hotels where they existed, not because the brothers were teetotal but because these hotels tended to be quieter and cheaper. They were not always available, however. Francis's letters to Isaac described both the boredom and the intrusion on privacy from which it was sometimes hard to escape. In 1850, he wrote: 'I am all by myself, for though I have no objection to society I dislike those of the drinking description who usually make the Sunday dinner an opportunity of taking an extra glass, as they would say, [sic] but an extra pint of wine.'[61] Sharing hotel accommodation with competitors' travellers, yet avoiding 'the drinking, swearing, fast commercial men' who dominated the commercial room, was an occupational burden, as was intermittent illness[62] which contributed further to the depressing experiences which the brothers related in their letters to Isaac.[63]

A combination of physical exhaustion, isolation, and disagreeable contacts contributed to the brothers' despondency, which Isaac sought to dispel in his letters. George, however, required more than sympathy and encouragement. That becomes clear from correspondence in 1850–1 which precipitated a managerial crisis.

Marketing management, family, and partnership: transition for growth

George presented his father (then aged 58) with a critical assessment of the management of the business. He described the direction as 'piecemeal', lacking co-ordination or collaboration between Isaac and his sons. He was also critical of Isaac's having ignored the possibility of illness and its effect on the business, urging the appointment of a trainee whose capabilities and integrity could be tried and tested before such an eventuality.[64] 'We should not have our business in such a high state of tension. We can hardly turn our heads round or look about us with an eye to the general good. We must, for the wheel will go round and crush us if we do.'[65] Thus began a process whereby the younger generation began to take increasing managerial control. George's criticisms of the conduct of the family firm have a modern ring:

> Often the ground has been discussed but never any decision taken on strategy, or if so written in the sand . . . I think we never sufficiently knew what we would be after, how far we intended to advertise, and what the means, to reap the benefit thereof . . . One of the main faults has been 'an unlimited democracy', our plans never starting from the beginning, were subjected to open counsel and debate.

George described this process as 'agreeable' but in the absence of a summing up, he felt that 'a firm spot of earth from chaos from which we could commence proceedings' was never established.[66]

Observing that Isaac had not the least idea of the objectives and overall strategy of the business, George urged him to initiate a detailed discussion (based on written documentation) regarding his intentions, as well as a thorough review of strategy and resources. George predicted that the addition of new lines combined with a policy of systematic advertising would enlarge the partnership's 'circle of ambition and the spokes of our activity'.[67] He argued that future growth and diversification necessitated a larger travelling staff, more managerial consultation, a closer supervision of workers to ensure a consistent quality of products advertised, and a more 'liberal agreement' (rewards), especially if expansion followed.[68]

George envisaged withdrawing from travelling (which Isaac had been unwilling to allow) to enable himself to assume an executive position as director in Hull. He also proposed a systematic reorganisation of selling activities, the Reckitt brothers concentrating on major towns for specific purposes, while agents served the country districts. London would receive special attention in the form of a 'missionary plan' which would involve going direct to the public by advertising and visiting washerwomen and housekeepers, a marketing strategy which was applicable to other major conurbations. 'A few years of these direct appeals will gain us some proportion of the public to our side.' Based on his experience on the road, he advised Isaac: 'The shopkeeper too often will not listen to you because your article is unknown and his customers do not ask for it, but we shall force the shopkeepers to get it for we shall talk over his customer . . . and he must then get it or let people go elsewhere.' Recognition by the jurors at the Great Exhibition of 1851 of the superiority of Reckitt's soluble starch was a welcome boost, though Colman's also achieved a similar mention. This publicity may have contributed to boosting already rising sales. In the previous year, George had urged upon Isaac the importance of ensuring swift delivery of orders: 'I work the men up to an honesty wish to push the article and then we allow them to cool down by the slowest process; let not this be.'[69]

Roughly a year after the policy was adopted, George expressed his dejection at 'finding the immense number of piles that want driving ere we laid a foundation'.[70] 'We must contrive steadily to work our way uphill . . . struggling amidst the deep gloom of early unsuccess.'[71] Further discouragement was occasioned by the absence from Isaac's letters of any reference to George's proposals for a reform of management structure and strategy.[72] Continuing illness led to George spending less time on the road and more in the Counting House, a situation which prompted the younger Francis to express his own views on the business. He echoed George's opinion that travelling was both the most difficult and most important part of their business in the sense that it was not routine. 'Now this travelling is distasteful to me and it is distasteful to George, but it is indispensable and it must be done';[73] though after having spent nearly seven years on the road he also expressed a reluctance 'almost amounting to an objection' to continuing.

Comparing George's annual sales with those of himself and James, he concluded that George was not pulling his weight, lagging behind by between £600 and £700. Correctly anticipating family differences, Francis requested a partnership agreement, though for three or four, rather than seven years, because 'in case of disagreement there should not be a barrier to separation which might possibly be advantageous'. Should his father disagree (to whom he gave an assurance that he wished not to give offence) he requested assistance in trying his fortune elsewhere.[74] There is a gap in the archive, which conceals the extent to which the proposal put to Isaac by his two eldest sons was implemented at that time. However, it is significant that Francis was admitted to the partnership a few months later in 1852. George was deputed to spearhead sales of black lead for polishing grates and stoves, a new addition to the product range.[75]

Issues of marketing strategy, selling, and salesmen

Isaac agreed to the appointment of an assistant traveller in 1850, though nearly two years passed before a suitable recruit could be found from extended family or Friends.[76] In 1852, William Barber, a Friend, approached Isaac with a view to selling Reckitt's products in London. This was a market the Reckitts had found difficult to penetrate because of the lack of interest shown by London agents who enjoyed close relations with the large, long-established London starch makers. Because of the firm's wider product range now on offer, Barber was given the chance at a salary of £200 plus 'liberal commission'. The arrangement was that he should deal exclusively in Reckitt products. He was warned to expect 'uphill, arduous work'.[77] To William Eason, who offered his services to sell in Ireland, Isaac gave the option of buying and selling Reckitt's starches or selling on commission with the provision that Eason would be held responsible for all debts. The arrangement reached was *del credere* commission whereby four months' credit was allowed on goods supplied, though on deposit of a security guarantee for the sum of £200. Commissions ranged between 10 and 15 per cent on different items.[78] Orders for washing paste and wheaten starch outran Reckitt's capacity to keep up, despite increasing the work force. Indeed, it is quite clear that advertising was not driven by a need to clear excess supply. The partners' problem in the 1850s was one of ensuring that production kept pace with orders. This resulted in the recruitment of more workers who included a clerk to keep the books up to date in order to avoid losing orders.[79]

The problem of meeting orders was exacerbated by product diversification. The sale of imported ultramarine for laundry blue began in 1852, as did that of black lead (ground graphite mixed with carbon black) purchased from de Beers. From 1855, Reckitt's produced black lead at the Hull factory

either as a liquid or paste.[80] The 1862 International Exhibition was important for the development of this trade because it publicised Sir Benjamin
Brodie's experiments producing blacking for polish.[81] George attributed
initial distribution difficulties to an unreliable resident London agent and
a lack of an established position from which to compete with Nixey, the
leader in the trade.[82] Improvement of the product by developing a puri-
fied formula coupled with heavy, concentrated advertising was the policy
adopted to break into this expanding trade.[83]

Intra-family disagreements regarding marketing strategy (particularly
over the recruitment of additional travellers) and the organisational structure of the business came to a head following Isaac's death in 1862.[84]
Henceforward, Frank, assisted by James, oversaw the business from Hull,
while George established a London Office in order to develop sales there
and in the Home Counties. Under the new system, each of the other travellers was allocated a regional sales territory from which he advised those
planning advertising in Hull.[85]

After a short period outside the business, George returned to the firm as
head of the London sales office and was a director in the restructured company from 1879. Meanwhile, in 1868, the appointment of Thomas Ferens
(aged 21) as correspondence clerk to James at Hull at £70 a year marked a
step forward in the Reckitts' marketing strategy. His prime responsibility was
to analyse the sales of the gradually increasing number of travellers (eight by
the 1870s), to make out their commission accounts, and keep a set of books.[86]

Effective commercial travellers were acknowledged to be a valuable
human resource. In the formative years of the business travellers were
given responsibility for opening accounts with retailers. Upon their judgement, therefore, depended the degree of financial risk to which the supplier
was exposed. Thus, Isaac's advice to the first non-family traveller: 'There
are plenty of good men without running the risk with doubtful ones . . .
Do not let their anxiety to sell with unsound money, better to send fewer
orders and safe for the former system will be sure to end in *loss* and *disap-
pointment* to both thee and ourselves. Unsafe men always order heavily.'[87]
Twenty years later, the Reckitts were still alert to the value of an effective
sales force. When two starchmaking firms failed, the Reckitt brothers were
quick to inquire whether they might be the source of good travellers. This
coincided with James's wish to replace the midland traveller 'who . . . does
not get around fast enough, is eccentric, and unimprovable'.[88] Recruitment
and management of salesmen required sensitivity, vigilance, and intervention. For example, in 1872, Francis wrote to George Baker with a view
to recruitment. Baker's considerable reputation as a salesman in the past
was, however, also accompanied by a tendency to indulge in less acceptable
behaviour which prompted this letter:

Respected Friend, We have been recommended to you by some of our mutual friends as wanting a situation . . . The present value of the birth is about £300 per annum after expenses. Payment is by commission. Removal from your present residence would be a necessity, you could then spend half your nights at home . . . You will excuse our making it a stipulation that if we accepted you as a traveller we should require you to take 'the pledge'; this may seem uncalled for but from what we have heard some time since it would be more satisfactory to both parties.

Baker showed little enthusiasm for the offer.[89] The salesman whose territory was the west of London also gave cause for concern: 'Do you think he requires more perseverance or is he naturally a defective traveller?'[90] Arrangements were made to replace him. When Reckitt's approached another 'respected Friend' to recommend a salesman for Scotland, the conditions were residence in Glasgow for one third of his time, the remainder to be spent travelling and sleeping in hotels at least four days a week. In fact, the person appointed was dismissed within months after twice absenting himself 'off drinking'. As guarantor, his brother was liable to pay compensation.[91] Another, who was described as having 'gone on the spree', had also caused offence among customers in the Channel Isles, in this instance his inebriated condition prompted a call to the police to remove him from the shop. Three years before, he had been removed from a guaranteed minimum payment contract on account of drink. On returning, his sales had doubled which made his lapse especially disappointing. He was reminded that having failed to keep his pledge he must undertake to renew it, to 'drop the drink completely . . . and stick to it – otherwise . . .'.[92] Managers monitored every kind of behaviour.[93]

Submitting false orders was a frequent reason for terminating employment as was selling stock under price, selling free samples, and making false claims for rent. In such cases a guarantor, usually a family member but sometimes an agency such as the Guardian Society, paid the deficit.[94] These misdemeanours, in addition to incompetence, carelessness, being too slow, or being 'a regular scamp' led to dismissals causing a high turnover in junior salesmen, thus underlining the importance of careful recruitment. Reckitt's managers sought to appoint men who were not 'reticent', who could offer more than 'a better class workman' could, and commented favourably on candidates who displayed respectability, gentlemanly style and dress, energy, and a capacity for hard work. An advertisement for a salesman which appeared in *The Grocer* in 1877 ran as follows: 'Wanted by an old-established English House who wish to increase their connections amongst grocers, a gentleman of energy and good address to represent them . . . security required.' Referees were asked whether an applicant was 'strictly honourable, sober, and of good moral character'.[95] The Reckitts also looked for relevant experience. Thus, an applicant who hitherto had sold flour was informed '. . . the trade you have been engaged in does not give you any experience in the sale of our goods, but rather the reverse, as although you may know something of the grocers and competition yet it requires so much more persuasion and talking to sell starches, blues and black leads than it does to sell flour, that we are not sure that one would not unfit you for the other.' He was engaged on trial and posted to the Isle of Man to test his mettle.[96]

In 1879, a new category of salesperson began to be deployed. The trigger appears to have been sales resistance to Paris Blue in the north of England where Ripley's blue was the principal competitor. The Leeds traveller reported 'Paris Blue is a dead letter among the small shops . . . The generality of the people are disloyal and don't care for advertised goods and especially if used by royalty'.[97] Sales there had halved since 1876, a development which coincided with a determined effort by Ripley to win over the small shopkeepers in the region to his rival blue.[98] The 'special travellers', appointed by the Reckitts on the suggestion of the salesman in whose territory Ripley was making headway, were initially referred to as 'sub-travellers' but subsequently became known as 'introducers'. Their task was to distribute showcards to small shops, help retailers with shop displays, ensure a prominent place for testimonials and other promotional matter, and to distribute free samples of Reckitt products to consumers, anticipating that thereafter they would call to place orders at the shops.[99] This formed the basis of a model strategy to supplement the selling activities of the senior travellers. Introducers also visited laundries to demonstrate how best to use Reckitt's products, and in calling on shops in order to show the products and describe their advantages, rather than to take orders.[100]

Another development of sales activity occurred simultaneously. In 1879, Payne, the Birmingham traveller, secured the Reckitts' agreement to his employing an assistant for whom he was willing to pay £100 plus travel expenses. Payne was to receive commission on the orders generated by the assistant. When Ferens appointed Read as the assistant traveller he described Payne to him as 'a gentlemanly and nice man whom we think you will get on with'. The agreement specified that the senior traveller would visit retailers once every six weeks; the assistant, once a quarter. Payne paid for the time spent by Read in calling on the regular trade, though the commission on any orders arising therefrom accrued to Payne. The partners paid for the time which they decided Read should spend in advertising-related activities and visiting.[101]

The willingness of the Birmingham traveller to employ his own assistant at £100 a year suggests that earnings from commission must have been substantial. Reckitt's travellers' annual salaries varied between £150 and

£350 (in some instances guaranteed by the partners) plus expenses of up to £1 a day.[102] In 1877, an applicant to become a senior traveller for Reckitt in the Scottish region (an area yielding only moderate sales) was offered £350 plus expenses, though it was assumed that he should be able to earn as much again on commission.[103] Total earnings of this magnitude are comparable with those received by Charles Lea of Huntley & Palmer, popularly known as 'King of the Commercial Travellers'. In 1874, his salary (he was not eligible for commission) was £750, that of his deputy £500, while the firm's other travellers (whom Corley has described as the 'aristocrats' among business employees in Victorian England) typically earned roughly £200 or so a year.[104] Comparisons with the civil service reveal Reckitt's salesmen to be receiving earnings roughly equivalent to those in the administrative grade, well above engineers employed in the service. The maximum for clerks at the Bank of England after 25 years' service was £300 plus, and in a provincial bank, £400; insurance company senior clerks reached maximum salaries of between £500 and £600. Measured by earnings, several of Reckitt's travelling salesmen, like some of their contemporaries in other trades, were clearly solidly 'middle-middle' rather than lower-middle class[105] as they have been presented by historians hitherto.[106]

Salesmen's levels of remuneration reflected their value not only in drumming up trade but as observers and communicators of intelligence regarding the tactics adopted by rivals. They were sources of advice as to how to counter such competition, whether through pricing policy, advertising, size of packets, or the packaging itself. In the marketing of household goods, the last two variables were of particular importance, not least because of the implications for branding and advertising and warrant further consideration.

Packaging products

It is not a coincidence that the makers and sellers of patent medicines and mineral waters and the makers of blacking compound were among the first to figure among the most active commercial advertisers. These products were sold only in bottles which, when labelled, could display the name of the maker or retailer or another symbol which the consumer could recognise and connect with wider forms of advertising in the newspapers or through trade cards issued to agents, wholesalers, and retailers. When dry goods began to be sold pre-packed to alleviate the difficulties of increasing the number of buyers, the number of widely advertised products increased.

The tea-dealers appear to have been first in this development, though there are no detailed accounts of their innovations. Quaker John Horniman began to sell packaged branded tea in 1826.[107] George Reckitt remarked upon the tea-dealers' marketing innovation in 1840 when he first began to travel.[108] In 1850, on the basis of several years' experience in selling 'on the road', George told his father Isaac Reckitt: 'I suspect shopkeepers of not always possessing the interest or spirit in winning over customers to our articles.' He advocated emulation of the tea-dealers' marketing methods by making a direct appeal to grocers through regular visits and by advertising.[109] The introduction of packaging using wrapping paper was of crucial importance to this strategy. In part, this development was stimulated by the mechanisation of paper production and the consequent increase in production capacity and speed in delivery which began to have an effect, beginning in the early 1830s.[110] The fall in production costs, the lowering of tariffs and reductions in Excise combined to bring about a fall in paper prices by 60 per cent, most of the fall occurring between the late 1820s and 1850. Furthermore, the quality and variety of machine-made paper for wrapping and printing improved, resulting in the production of superior finish, strength, and regularity.[111] The introduction of cylinder printing further enhanced the quality while reducing the cost of packaging.[112]

The value to manufacturers of these developments is implied in the instructions given by Isaac to the firm's supplier of printed packaging in 1851: 'We note that several manufacturers are packing their starch in small packets upon printed paper which saves the trouble and expense of labels.' He ordered wrapping paper for 2oz orders 'got up in a pretty and tempting style at the same time to cost as little as possible'. He pointed out that strong paper would be required to prevent splitting in the process of packaging and that speedy delivery was essential. 'We want to thank you for your lowest price as most probably our consumption could be large, possibly very large.'[113] No cost data for the period have survived, though in the1860s, expenditure on paper and labels added 15 per cent to the production cost of Reckitt's starch products; the cost of cases, boxes, and tins for biscuits accounted for roughly 35 per cent of the revenue from sales.[114] Isaac took immense trouble to ensure that packaging was attractive and effective, advising the stationers on text, substance, colours, and lettering. In preparation for the launch of the new Patent Wheaten Starch in 1850, Isaac explained his packaging requirements to the stationer: 'Thou must make the colour as deep and good as thou can and the gloss as great, but it must be proceeded with without delay.'[115] Novelty was perceived to be all-important, not only in the quality, size, and shape of the product lines but in packaging. In the 1870s, sales increased when starch was sold in boxes complete with different pretty pictures on each. Later, blue wrapped in distinctively designed striped flannel was introduced as 'bag blue' to compete with Edge's similarly presented 'dolly blue' which had established a market in the north of England.[116]

'. . . surpasses any other . . . incomparably the best':
advertising policies and practice

Originally developed to sell mustard, Colman's marketing methods were highly regarded by his competitors, notably his making direct contacts with retailers through travellers, introducing attractive packages, and advertising on a large scale through printed trade cards. In 1849, George Reckitt, then aged 24 and a partner in the reconstituted Isaac Reckitt & Sons (formed in 1848), had spent most of the previous five years out on the road. He admired the Colmans' practice 'of sending numberless small counterbills which I fear we neglect, and he also sends to good customers one or two of his showcards handsomely enclosed in a gilt frame with plate glass and it, of course, then takes an honorary position in the window; from what I see I am afraid we are somewhat behind hand in these little means of attracting attention. Directly I arrive home we must set to work about these matters.'[117]

Deeply in debt in a business which continued to be barely profitable, Isaac agreed to allow Francis, aged 16, to go on the road in order to reduce commission payments to agents to whom initially sales had been entrusted. Saving their salaries was necessary to avoid insolvency, as was the development of a product sufficiently distinctive to justify imitating Colman's approach to marketing. In 1849, Jeremiah Colman had applied this approach to marketing a new product line, Colman's Patent Rice Starch, about which George remarked, 'He braggs a great deal of it.'[118]

This association between a novel product, modification or extension of a product line, advertising, and travelling salesmen, quickly became characteristic of the trade in starch. Colman's had developed this approach to sell mustard following a report from a commercial traveller named Copeman (aged 22) who had been sent to America to select 'safe men' as dealers. He suggested that it might be commercially advantageous 'to identify Colman's mustard with the consumer'. Jeremiah Colman proceeded to implement this idea, introducing showcards, tin containers, and paper wrapping for both mustard and starch.[119] The bull's head logo, red on a yellow background, advertising Colman's mustard was used as the firm's first trademark in 1855,[120] as was Reckitt's Azure Blue.

Beginning in1848, George Reckitt's concern to develop novel products, defined by size as well as quality, was coupled with a conviction that effective advertising was equally crucial in withstanding competition. 'In the system of advertising we are about to improvise, we are taking the surest means of effecting and gaining a connection by the fact of directness and certainty of its principles. We are going to those who after all is said and done decide the fate of an article . . . we shall be first in the field . . . I trust a few years of these direct appeals will gain us some portion of the public on our side.'[121] Francis, too, was convinced: 'if we do go the whole hog in advertising and do the thing well, we shall get ultimately repaid.'[122] The financial background to the decision to advertise is obscure. After seven unprofitable years, in 1847, a trading profit of £1000 and another of £1700 the following year enabled the partners to begin to repay heavy loan commitments entered into to start the business. However, bad debts offset trading success; in 1851, bad debts reduced a trading profit of £1000 to £650.[123] Loan capital was a continuing burden until it was cleared in 1858.[124] Despite these difficulties, the achievement of profitability provided Isaac with sufficient confidence to be optimistic about the future. Both George and Francis argued that the costs of advertising were necessary to counter competition, and particularly to challenge the large long-established starchmakers in London.[125]

The plan, agreed in 1848, was to advertise Frederic's new double refined Patent Soluble Starch partly through the press, partly by distributing showcards and counterbills to grocers, and partly by a house-to-house delivery of handbills. The large cities in the north of England were the first to be targeted.[126] Frustrated by Isaac's apparent slowness to support the new patent starches in Hull, George (from his northern territory) questioned his father's commitment, observing that unless the plan were introduced within a year there would be no point in proceeding with it.[127] Meanwhile, Isaac sought to elicit a testimonial from the Imperial Laundry of Nicholas, Emperor of Russia, for the purpose of advertising. This was achieved by dispatching a consignment to St Petersburg. After a year's silence, a reply was forthcoming from the Russian Consulate General. He praised 'in the highest terms' the superiority of Patent Wheaten Starch 'to any I have ever been able to procure for the use of the royal family'. It was stronger, more economical 'whilst it gives an incomparable colour and brilliancy and an enduring gloss finish such as I never witnessed from starch before'.[128] Thereafter, counterbills referred to Reckitt's Patent and Imperial Starch manufactured by 'Starch Manufacturers to his Imperial Majesty of all the Russias'.[129] A similar approach to secure a testimonial from the Emperor Louis Napoleon III followed. Both appeared in an advertisement headed 'A LIST OF DISTINC-TIONS conferred on ISAAC RECKITT & SON, Starch Manufacturers, Hull', as did a reference to The Great Exhibition award for the superiority of Patent Soluble Starch. 20,000 circulars and 100,000 handbills were ordered for distribution to convey this message to retailers and consumers.[130]

Several times Isaac instructed the printers to devise advertisements which were handsome, which included 'shaped' lettering or novel bordering, mixing colour in ways which would maximise legibility: 'our article demands a card . . . whose novel appearance from the novelty of design, colouring and ensemble is striking at first sight.'[131] Texts used in advertisements varied.

Some were intended to instruct potential users as to the advantages of the product. For example, one stressed labour saving and simplicity for users of soluble starch and included a hint of knocking copy: 'The position that this article has so long held is the best testimonial of its invaluable qualities: brilliancy, gloss, facility with which it can be made . . . requires no boiling, scarcely any clapping and does not adhere to the iron, imparting a lustrous finish far different from that given by the half-made clammy powder starches.'[132]

Another claimed that 'the use of Reckitt's improved washing compound . . . saved time, labour, and money and the wear and tear of rubbing'; another emphasised purity and crystal transparency which prevented discoloration, and a 'brilliant delicate whiteness unobtainable from any other starch'.[133]

Complementing this essentially informative approach to advertising was an attempt to employ images intended to appeal to the consumer through association with the effect which the product was predicted to have. Others presented images which suggested by association alone. In 1851, inspired by Glenfield's showcard which included the female form, Isaac Reckitt commissioned an advertisement in which the three graces figured prominently. Isaac explained to the printer: '. . . the Graces are not necessarily connected with our business, but we thought that if dressed in white and wreathed in lace, falling in graceful festoons about them, there would be an appositeness combined with novelty which would be attractive.' He criticised sample images: the graces were 'not light or aerial enough' and although 'draped are hardly sufficiently so'.[134] In a circular intended for wide distribution the Reckitts gave an assurance: 'Being determined to bring it [soluble starch] within the reach of all classes they supply it at such low prices to the retailer as enables him to sell it even in small packets at 6d per lb.'[135] Such showcards, circulars, and counterbills (nearly 100,000 in 1851) were distributed to each of the grocers who stocked Reckitt's starches. The names of the retailers recording the highest turnovers were given an additional boost as their names were printed with the advertisements.[136] Wall advertising began in 1850.[137]

The Reckitts were among the first to explore the value of services offered by the newly emerging profession of advertising agents. They were also quick to learn that before paying the high charges demanded for newspaper insertions, it was sensible to ensure beforehand that they appeared in a position which would justify the expenditure. Henceforward a continuing element in marketing, it may have been newspaper and magazine advertising which led Reckitt's to dispense with London agents in favour of the appointment of London travellers and direct sales to grocers. Their supplies were dispatched thrice weekly by steamboat from Hull.[138]

Such was the plan of campaign when Paris Blue was launched in 1870. Introducers distributed free samples to all London laundresses. Newspaper advertising, 'not in an extravagant manner but sufficient to make a stir in the trade in London', was placed in *The Graphic, The Mirror, The News of the World, Lloyds' Weekly, The Sunday Times* and *Punch. The Weekly Budget,* a penny newspaper with between 200,000 and 300,000 circulation was another vehicle for Reckitt advertising.[139] The Reckitts were conscious of the importance of directing their appeals to women. In addition to 'ladies' papers', Reckitt advertisements for starch and blue were placed in *Lett's Family Washing Book* which was one of the early specialist housekeeping advice manuals about to become widely distributed to the households of the middle classes. In 1873, Reckitt's own washing book went into print. The initial distribution numbered 100,000 for London and the same for other targeted areas. Included among the washing tips were 13 advertisements; those intended for the lady of the house placed on the right, those directed to the laundresses on the left.[140] Initially, these washing books, of which there were 2d and 6d versions, were sold to grocers by salesmen at a profit. However, the publication was so successful that a book hawker was employed to sell from door to door. The London book trade took copies at cost price.[141] A grocer's handbook followed, aimed particularly at retailers in the country towns and villages who were beyond sight of the billboards and buses of the cities. The Reckitts' philosophy was 'to constantly keep our name before both the consumers and dealers', a policy which included targeting one quarter of all omnibuses and carts in London to become moving sites for advertising Reckitt products.[142]

The origins of modern marketing: proprietary household goods in the mid-nineteenth century

This article set out to pose the following questions: when, why, how, and with what effect were modern marketing methods (defined as branding, sustained direct selling, and advertising products to a wide spectrum of consumers (though excluding systematic product development) introduced? In some important respects the answers run counter to the conventional interpretations of the history of marketing outlined in section 1. Historians are interested in origins as well as representativeness. It seems that tea-merchants were the first innovators. Although their marketing activities are not recorded in any detail, their influence through diffusion is attested by the early experience of John Cadbury and Francis Frean, both of whom began their business careers in the tea trade. Further evidence is that supplied by George Reckitt who in the 1840s specifically singled out the tea-merchants as having been at the forefront of marketing. Histories of the tea trade contain few details of this process. Similarly Colman's innovativeness in the mustard and starch trades during the mid-nineteenth century is poorly documented because of huge archival gaps. By contrast, the relative richness of the archives of the forerunners of Reckitt & Colman plc makes it possible to answer each of the questions posed in the introduction with respect to these manufacturers of proprietary household goods. We do not claim that the Reckitts were the first to practise modern marketing methods as defined in the introduction, but undoubtedly they were among the first and their history is well documented.

Several conclusions emerge from this case study, which have a wider relevance for the history of marketing. First, modern marketing methods were introduced well before those of the chocolate makers in the 1860s, let alone those of Lever twenty years later.[143] The first innovators of modern marketing methods were tea-merchants, whose history is poorly documented, and manufacturers of spices and starch. The circumstances surrounding the marketing of mustard are obscure. Innovations by starch makers occurred in specific historical circumstances when the proliferation of 'patent' starches during the 1840s followed the removal of state monopolistic control and the deregulation of the trade. In the case of direct selling, the innovations were developed partly to counter the divided loyalties of intermediary agents and to push sales. In the case of branding and advertising, the intention was to activate a pull factor whereby potential consumers communicated their demand preferences to retailers.

Second, product development was central to business strategy. The Reckitts were conscious of their intention to create consumer demand for a product which had a long history as a commercially traded product stretching back into the sixteenth century, though widespread use originated at the end of the eighteenth century.[144] Isaac and his sons read correctly the implications of a changed economic and social environment and the opportunities for creating a much greater consumer demand. The driving imperative to act, however, was the prospect before Isaac of yet another business failure. Reckitt's business records show that throughout the 1840s and early 1850s the firm was barely profitable and deeply in debt through loans incurred in starting up the enterprise. New product development (indeed novelty of any kind so long as grocers or chemists and druggists sold the product) was seen as a route to escape financial difficulties. As part of the drive to profitability product development included the substitution of raw materials to give the option of lower prices or higher profit margins. In that process, trial and error was characteristic of Frederic's numerous experiments in an attempt to transform his own ideas or those of his father and brothers into commercial innovations.[145] Supporting these with systematic advertising and direct selling was a policy adopted, not to clear excess production but to increase sales in competition with other makers, to enlarge vitally important cash flow, and subsequently, to establish an expanded core business. Expanding production (sales tripled between 1861 and 1874)[146] presented difficulties primarily in securing raw materials, though that was a cyclical rather than a long term problem. The Reckitts imported blue for resale under the Reckitt brand until 1884, a development which marked a step shift in the knowledge of industrial chemistry required of managers.[147]

Third, the important early marketing innovations introduced by these manufacturers occurred while they were SMEs. From the mid-1850s, the success of the new marketing policies created a problem; at times sales growth tended to outpace production. Turnover increased from £8000 in 1851 to £21,742 in 1861. During the 1860s, the success of Reckitt's Diamond Black Lead and the new rice starch saw sales rise to £36,307 and to twice that by 1876.[148] Exports also date from this period. The evidence from Reckitt's history suggests that the youthful sales team regarded the cost incurred in advertising and packaging to be a necessary condition of entry into competition with the larger and longer established leaders of the trade. In that respect advertising costs were no different from the (relatively small) capital requirements to enter into the trade. Numbers employed were similarly small during the middle decades when the aforementioned marketing innovations took place. Reckitt's workers increased from about 25 when business commenced in 1840 to perhaps 100 by 1851, and to between 200 and 300 by 1868. Colman's work force rose from between 30 and 40 in the 1830s to roughly 100 in 1851; they rose from between 500 and 600 by 1861 to about 1000 by 1869.[149]

Fourth, the methods of selling and advertising were modern in the sense that they were part of a planned strategy which related product development to branding, selling by relatively highly paid travellers, and advertising. The novel 'grand scheme', as the brothers called it, consisted of establishing standard brands through steady, systematic, and continuous advertising city by city. Furthermore, while product development focused primarily on creating demand through novelty and establishing brand names among middle class consumers, this approach was complemented by a policy of introducing low priced packets advertised directly to the working classes. The content of advertisements also anticipated the increasingly common trend towards the end of the century to seek to manipulate consumers through associational, rather than literal images. Emphasis upon the articles' use value and economy, either of time, effort, or money was accompanied by allusions to their effect on lifestyle. Reckitt's promotion of cleanliness, especially 'dazzling whiteness', which anticipated Lever's soap campaigns a generation later, was a direct appeal to actual or aspirations to respectability. Contrary to impressions conveyed by conventional accounts, neither purveyors of patent medicines nor soap makers spearheaded marketing modernity, but blenders of tea and manufacturers of mustard and starch. The

Reckitts were quick to emulate and to develop their methods further. At the same time, by promoting the growth of the starch, blue, and polish trades which they came to dominate the Reckitts were responding to and reinforcing the cleanliness dimension in Victorian values.

Finally, the transformation of marketing described above was the achievement of an organisation in which the key innovators were the family partners. They planned strategies, implemented them on their travels and later exercised close control of a carefully selected group of salesmen. Because product diversification and development was determined, as a matter of policy, by concentrating on the exploitation of a distribution network confined to grocers (though later also through agents overseas), the transfer of marketing techniques from one product to another did not present a problem. Thus, despite internal tensions and some failures, a coherent product strategy conceived and conducted under family control and management was central to the nineteenth century foundations of the firm's longstanding competitive advantage.

Notes

* We are grateful to the Leverhulme Trustees for funding the research on which this article is based (F/204/R 1997–2000). We are also indebted to Mr Basil Reckitt who allowed access to private family papers (referred to below as BRFP). The archives of Reckitt & Colman located in Hull are referred to as R & C. Those referring to the Reckitt enterprise are prefixed with R followed by the number given by the company archivist, Mr Gordon Stephenson, to whom we express our thanks for his extremely valuable advice and assistance. We also acknowledge our debt to Reckitt and Colman plc for permission to research the companies' records.

1 A. D. Chandler Jr, *Scale and Scope: The Dynamics of Industrial Capitalism* (Cambridge Mass: Belknapp Press, 1994), pp. 262–3.
2 R. Fitzgerald, *Rowntree and the Marketing Revolution, 1862–1969* (Cambridge: CUP, 1995), p. 24.
3 Fitzgerald, *Rowntree*, p. 24.
4 Edward Ellison, 'The story of Pears', *Progress*, 41 (1950–1), pp. 18–19.
5 Lever commenced soap manufacture in 1885. Charles Wilson, *The History of Unilever: A Study in Economic Growth and Social Change* Vol. I (London: Cassell, 1954), pp. 27–32.
6 R. Fitzgerald, 'Employers' labour strategies, industrial welfare, and the response to New Unionism at Bryant & May, 1888–1930', *Business History*, 31 (1989), pp. 48–65.
7 Chandler, *Scale and Scope*, pp. 260–4; Fitzgerald, *Rowntree*, p. 27.
8 McKendrick has presented Josiah Wedgwood as a pioneer in marketing. It is true that several of the methods which he adopted share common elements with those defining the 'modern marketing' characteristic of a later period. However, Wedgwood's appeal specifically to a luxury market and to the status aspirations of the middling classes is an important difference. N. McKendrick,

'Josiah Wedgwood: An eighteenth century entrepreneur in salesmanship and marketing techniques', *Econ. Hist. Rev.*, 12 (1959/60), pp. 408–33; idem, 'Commercialisation and the economy', in McKendrick et al, *The Birth of a Consumer Society: The Commercialisation of Eighteenth Century England* (1982), pp. 290–3. For a dissenting evaluation of Wedgwood's role in this context see L. Weatherill, *Consumer Behaviour and Material Culture in Britain 1660–1815* (New York: Garland, 1986) and B. Fine and E. Leopold, 'Consumerism and the industrial revolution', *Social History*, 15 (1990), pp. 151–79. See also W. H. Fraser, *The Coming of the Mass Market* (London: Hambledon, 1981); T. A. B. Corley, *Quaker Enterprise in Biscuits: Huntley & Palmers of Reading, 1822–1972* (London: Hutchinson, 1972); idem, 'Consumer marketing in Britain, 1914–1960', *Business History*, XIX (1987), pp. 65–83; O. Westall, 'The competitive environment of British industry, 1850–1914', in M. Kirby and M. Rose (eds), *Modern Business Enterprise in Britain* (London: Routledge, 1994), pp. 207–35.

9 For a critical overall view of historians' treatment of marketing see Roy Church, 'New perspectives on the history of products, firms, marketing and consumers in Britain and the United States since the mid-nineteenth century', *Econ. Hist. Rev.*, LII (1999), pp. 405–35.

10 Whom Fitzgerald cites, *Rowntree*, p. 37.

11 S. Diaper, 'J. S. Fry & Sons', in C. Harvey and J. Press (eds), *Studies in the Business History of Bristol* (Bristol, 1988), p. 38.

12 T. R. Nevett, *Advertising in Britain* (London: Heinemann for the History of Advertising Trust, 1981), pp. 31, 36.

13 Corley, 'Consumer marketing', p. 29.

14 V. Berridge, 'Popular journalism and working class attitudes, 1854–1886. A study of Reynold's newspapers and Lloyds weekly paper' (Unpublished PhD thesis, University of London, 1976), p. 24.

15 D. A. Simmons, *Schweppes, the First 200 Years* (London: Springwood Books, 1983), pp. 27–48.

16 Diaper, *Fry*, pp. 37–8.

17 Diaper, *Fry*, pp. 40, 44–5.

18 Corley, *Quaker Enterprise*, pp 37–8.

19 Corley, *Quaker Enterprise*, pp. 62–3, 73. Both Fry and Cadbury relied heavily on agents who, in the latter case, were dealt with through a London advertising agent for most of the nineteenth century.

20 Corley, 'Consumer marketing', p. 161.

21 Fitzgerald, *Rowntree*, p. 24; Fraser, *Mass Market*; Westall, 'Competitive environment'.

22 Williams, *Cadbury*, pp. 37–40.

23 G. Wagner, *Chocolate Conscience* (London: Chatto and Windus, 1987), pp. 33–4.

24 Diaper, *Fry*, p. 40.

25 N. Alexander and G. Akehurst (eds), *The Emergence of Modern Retailing 1750–1950* (London: Cass, *Business History* Special issue, 40 (1998).

26 Roy Church and Christine Clark, 'Cleanliness next to godliness: Christians in Victorian business', *Economic and Business History* (September, 1999).

27 Church and Clark, 'Cleanliness next to godliness'.

28 B. W. Peckham, 'Technological change in the British and French starch industries, 1750–1850', *Technology and Culture*, 27 (1986), pp. 25–9.

29 Peckham, 'British and French starch industries', pp. 20–3.
30 Anon, *A New System of Practical Domestic Economy* (1827), pp. 397–430;
   Eighth Report of the Commissioners of Inquiry into the Excise Establishment:
   Starch (PP 1834, XXV), p. 513.
31 Peckham, 'British and French starch industries', pp. 18–39.
32 Ibid., pp. 25–9.
33 D. Chapman-Huston, *Sir James Reckitt, A Memoir* (London: Faber and Gwire,
   1927), p. 109.
34 Basil N. Reckitt, *The History of Reckitt and Sons, Limited* (Hull: Brown, 1952),
   p. 8.
35 BRFP Vol. I, Francis to Frederic, 4 Jan. 1847.
36 Reckitt, *History*, p. 11.
37 BRFP, Vol. I, 1847 (nd); George to Isaac, 12 Nov. 1848.
38 BRFP, Vol. II, Isaac to George, 10 Oct. 1849.
39 BRFP, Appendix VII, Statement by George Reckitt (1860s?).
40 BRFP, Vol. II, George to Isaac, 14 Jan. 1850.
41 BRFP, Vol. II, George to Isaac, 23 April 1850.
42 Reckitt, *History*, p. 18.
43 Chicken, 'Ultramarine: a Case Study' (Unpublished PhD thesis, Open University, 1993), pp. 18–20, 108.
44 BRFP, Vol. III, George to Isaac, 22 April 1850.
45 BRFP, Vol. III, Isaac to George, 20 April 1850.
46 E. B. Southwell, 'J & J. Colman Ltd. Early days at Stoke Holy Cross', *Carrow Works Magazine*, XIX (October, 1925), p. 8.
47 E. B. Southwell, 'Looking backward', *Carrow Works Magazine*, XIII (January, 1920), p. 47.
48 BRFP, Vol. II, Isaac to George, 24 June, 14 Nov. 1847.
49 BRFP, Appendix VII, 'Statement' by George Reckitt (1864?); Reckitt, *History*, p. xv.
50 BRFP, Vol. II, Isaac to George, 18 Sept., 14 Nov. 1847.
51 BRFP, Vol. II, Isaac to George, 26 April 1847.
52 BRFP, Vol. II, Isaac to George 4 March 1846; Isaac to Frederic 29 Sept. 1846.
53 BRFP, Vol. II, Isaac to George, 18 and 28 Sept. 1847.
54 Reckitt, *History*, p. 12.
55 BRFP, Vol. II, George to Isaac, 16 July 1847.
56 Quoted in Reckitt, *History*, p. 17.
57 BRFP, Vol. II, 26 May 1849; Vol. III 14 Jan. 1850.
58 BRFP, Vol. III, George to Isaac, 23 April 1850.
59 Reckitt, *History*, pp. 15–16.
60 George described Hartlepool as 'a miserable hell hole of a place, the population are all low and rather humble – not great starch users.' From Bristol he wrote of his 'want of success [which] arises from the slowness of the people'. BRFP Vol. II, George to Isaac, 14 Jan. 1850; 23 Feb. 1849.
61 BRFP, Vol. II, 23 Nov. 1850.
62 Isaac suffered from rheumatism and neuritis for many years; James was similarly afflicted. Chapman-Huston, *Sir James*.
63 BRFP Frederic to Isaac, 23 Nov. 1850, James to Isaac, 16 March 1852.
64 BRFP, Vol. III, George to Isaac, 22 April 1850.
65 BRFP, Vol. III, George to Isaac, 22 April 1850.
66 BRFP, Vol. III George to Isaac, 20 April 1850.
67 BRFP, Vol. III George to Isaac, 22 April 1850.

68 BRFP, Vol. III, George to Isaac, 20 April 1850.

69 BRFP, Vol. II, George to Isaac, 2 Feb. 1850.

70 BRFP, Vol. II, George to Isaac, 18 March 1851.

71 BRFP, Vol. II, George to Isaac, 20 March 1851.

72 BRFP, Vol. III, 20 April 1850.

73 BRFP, Vol. III, Francis to Isaac, 1852 (nd).

74 BRFP, Vol. III, Francis to Isaac, 1852 (nd).

75 BRFP, Vol. III, Francis to George, 29 April 1853.

76 The terms for 'an energetic young man' were £100 salary plus 15/- daily expenses. BFRP Vol. III, Isaac to George, 25 April 1850.

77 Reckitt & Colman Business Archives (hereafter R & C), R 289, Letter book, Isaac to W. Barber, 27 Jan. 1852.

78 R & C, R 289, Isaac Reckitt's Letter book, 6 Feb. 1852.

79 BRFP, Vol. III, George to Isaac, 11 Nov. 1854.

80 Reckitt, *History*, p. 22.

81 Chapman-Huston, *Sir James*, pp. 60–1.

82 BRFP Vol. III, Francis to George, 29 April 1853.

83 BRFP, Vol. III, Francis to George, 29 April 1853.

84 Isaac willed the business to his three sons in equal shares. However, the difficulties of working together led George to withdraw from the partnership, taking his share in cash. This presented problems for the business which were resolved only by the intervention of the local Committee of Friends acting as arbitrators. Friend George March wrote to George Reckitt, expressing the view that it would be 'far better than resorting to the intricacies of the law, which I fear will not solve your difficulties and involve fearful expense. I desire a solution which tends to unite rather than widen the breach.' The upshot was that George left the partnership by agreement with his brothers, taking his third share which amounted to £16,000 in cash by stages under arbitration. The agreement precluded him from entering upon any of the business activities, directly or indirectly, then being carried on by Reckitt & Sons. BRFP, Vol. IV, Memorandum, Francis and James to George, 8 March 1864; S. Priestman to George, 14 March 1864.

85 BRFP, Vol. III, James to George, 12 Jan., J. Newborn to George, 14 July 1864.

86 BRFP Vol. IV, 14 July 1864; R & C, R 15, T. Ferens Copying book, f 164, 1880; B. Reckitt, 'On the road in the 1850s', *Ours*, 7 (May, 1926). By 1870, Ferens's annual salary was £135. When he was on the road he received an additional 4 per cent commission on starch and 8 per cent on blue sales. He became works manager in 1874 at a salary of £300 plus a share of the profits. In 1879, he became company secretary of the newly formed Reckitt & Sons Ltd. Elected to the Board in 1888, subsequently he became chairman in a company which was still owned and controlled by the Reckitt family. T. R. Ferens, *Ours* 7 (May 1926).

87 R & C, R 289, Isaac to W. Barber, 31 Jan. 1852.

88 R & C, R8, IRS Copying book, Francis and James to George, 31 Aug 1872, 28 Sept. 1872.

89 R & C, R8, IRS Copying book, Francis to G. Baker, 14 and 25 Nov. 1872.

90 R & C, R9 IRS Copying book, Francis to George, 32 Feb. 1874.

91 R & C, R9, IRS Copying book, Francis and James to George, 3 July, 12 Nov. 1877, 15, and 16 Feb. 1878.

92 R & C, R141, Isaac Reckitt & Sons (hereafter IRS), Board minute book, 24 July 1879; Ferens Copying book, 13 May, 1 June 1882.

93 For example, in 1881 Thomas Ferens wrote to Alexander as follows:
    We have several times from various sources since you began to travel for us
    had our attention drawn to the style of your dress and address, and although
    it is rather a delicate matter to mention, we think it better to advise you to be
    simpler and plainer in both respects. You will find that by cultivating a more
    open and friendly style with your customers that you will get on better terms
    with them than by being somewhat reticent and exclusive. We believe that if
    you adopt our suggestion that it will be to our mutual profit.
    P. S. Perhaps if you will excuse our noting that your use of an eyeglass instead
    of spectacles has, we believe, given offence to some of our customers.
    The letter ended by drawing attention to his relatively poor and declining
    orders. R & C, R15, Ferens Copying book, Ferens to Alexander, 8 Dec. 1881.
    Yet another was reported to have 'simply made his journey a course of dissipa-
    tion' resulting in a deficit in cash takings'. Ibid.
94 R & C, R71, IRS Personnel appointments.
95 R & C, R9 IRS Copying book, 8 Nov. 1877.
96 R & C, R9, IRS Copying book, to J Cousin 26 Sept. and 4 Oct. 1878.
97 R & C, R15, Ferens Copying book, 5 March 1881.
98 R & C R15, Ferens Copying book, 5 March 1881.
99 R & C, R15, Ferens Copying book, 7 March 1881; R9, IRS Copying book, 3
    Feb. 1879.
100 R & C, R9, IRS Copying book, 12 Feb; 11 and 14 March, 9 Aug 1879.
101 R & C, R9, IRS Copying book, Ferrens to Read, 5 Dec. 1879, 5 Dec. 1878, 3
    Jan. 1880.
102 R & C, R71 Personnel appointments.
103 R & C, R9, IRS Copying book, 8 Nov. 1877.
104 Corley, *Huntley & Palmer*, pp. 63, 73. In 1875, the chief traveller for Bodding-
    ton's brewery was paid £505 plus bonus. T. R. Gourvish and R. G. Wilson, *The
    British Brewing Industry* (Cambridge: CUP, 1994), p. 204.
105 Using the figures produced by Dudley Baxter for 1867, Bedarida classifies
    those earning between £300 and £1000 as belonging to the 'middle, middle
    class', *A Social History of Britain* (London: Routledge, 1991), p. 217.
106 C. P. Hosgood, 'The "Knights of the Road"; commercial travellers and the
    culture of the commercial room in late Victorian and Edwardian England',
    Victorian Studies (1994), pp. 519–47.
107 D. Forrest, *Tea for the British* (London: Chatto and Windus, 1973), pp.
    133–55.
108 BRFP, Vol. I, George to Isaac, 14 Jan., 30 April, and 16 Nov. 1840.
109 BRFP, Vol. III, George to Isaac, 20 Apr. 1850.
110 D. C. Coleman, *The British Paper Industry, 1495 to 1860* (Cambridge: CUP,
    1958), pp. 199, 202–3.
111 Coleman, *Paper Industry*, p. 205.
112 A. E. Musson, *The Typographical Association: Organisation and History up to
    1949* (Oxford: OUP, 1954), pp. 79–89.
113 R & C., R 289, Isaac Reckitt's Letter book, to Currie, Mackay & Kirkwood, 14
    Apr. 1851.
114 R & C, R11, Stocktaking ledger f3, f13.
115 R & C, R 289, Isaac Reckitt, General letter book, to BH, 22 April 1850.
116 R & C, R141, IRS Directors' minute book, 8 Dec. 1886.
117 BRFP, Vol. I, George to Isaac, 19 June 1849.

118 BRFP, Vol. I, 26 May 1849.
119 Colman Archives, Carrow Road, Norwich (now presumed to be located with Unilever Historical Archives, Port Sunlight); Jeremiah Colman to John Copeman, 1840.
120 *The Advertising Art of J. & J. Colman Ltd* (privately printed, 1977), p. 7.
121 Quoted in Reckitt, *History*, p. 19. George did, however, acknowledge that Anderson and Glenfield had already begun to advertise starch. George's innovation was to target advertising in certain cities and towns when travellers were present in those places ready to call on retailers to reinforce the effect of advertising.
122 BRFP, Vol. III, Francis to Isaac, 1850; Reckitt, 'On the Road in 1850', pp. 227–8.
123 Reckitt, *History*, pp. 10, 16.
124 Reckitt, *History*, p. 97.
125 Church and Clark, 'Cleanliness, competition'.
126 Reckitt, *History*, p. 17; R & C, R289 Isaac Reckitt Letter book, Isaac to W. Little, 2 July 1851; Isaac to Jackson & Asquith, 26 Dec. 1850; Isaac to Henry Reckitt, 10 May 1850; BRP 1850.
127 BRFP Vol. III, George to Isaac, 23 April 1850.
128 R & C, R289, Isaac Reckitt Letter book, St Petersburg Imperial Laundry to Isaac, 10 July 1850.
129 R & C, R289, Isaac Reckitt Letter book, Isaac to Cousin, 25 June 1850.
130 R & C. R289, Isaac Reckitt to Jackson and Asquith, 26 Dec. 1850; 14 Nov. 1851.
131 R & C, R289, Isaac Reckitt Letter book, Isaac to Mackay & Currie, 18 Nov. 1850.
132 R&C, R289, Isaac Reckitt Letter book, advertisement for *Stamford and Rutland Mercury* 2 Aug. 1851.
133 R & C., R289, Isaac Reckitt Letter book, advertisement for Mackay and Kirkward, 7 June 1851; Isaac to Jackson & Asquith, 3 May 1851.
134 R & C, R289, Isaac Reckitt Letter book, to Currie & Kirkward 24 Jan. 1851, 23 Apr. 1851.
135 R & C, R289, Isaac Reckitt Letter book, 3 Mar. 1851, I to Jackson & Asquith.
136 R & C, R289, Isaac Reckitt Letter book, Isaac to Johnson & Alloy 20 Aug., 15 Sept. 1851.
137 R & C, R289, Isaac Reckitt Letter book, to Currie, Mackay and Westwood, 7 May 1850, to Waterloo & Son, 14 August 1850.
138 R & C, R289, Isaac Reckitt Letter book, to advertising agent 10 Sept.; to Harvests 14 Oct. 1850.
139 R & Colman, R8, IRS Copying book, 24 Nov 72, 16 Oct. 1873; R9, IRS copying book, 12 Sept 1874.
140 R & C, R9, IRS Copying book, 12 April 1874; R8, IRS Copying book, 9 Dec. 1872, 13 Feb 1873.
141 R & C, R8, IRS Copying book, 22 Feb., 20 March, 12 Nov. 1873, 24 Dec. 1873.
142 R & C, R8, IRS Copying book, 13 Mar. 1873, 24 Oct. 72.
143 Charles Wilson, *The History of Unilever* Vol. I (London: Cassell, 1954), pp. 25–9.
144 Peckham, 'The British and French starch industries', pp. 18–39.
145 Reckitt, *History*, pp. 11–12.
146 R & C, J. B. Upton 'Reckitt's UK Sales, 1861–1954'.

32   *Roy Church and Christine Clark*

147 Reckitt, *History*, p. 22; Chicken, 'Ultramarine: A Case Study', p. 116.
148 R & C, J. B. Upton, 'Reckitt's UK Sales, 1861–1954'.
149 Chapman-Huston, p. 119; Reckitt, *History*, pp. 97–9; H. C. Colman, *Jeremiah James Colman, A Memoir* (London: 1905, pp. 90, 136); E. B. Southwell, 'J. & J. Colman Ltd. Early days at Stoke Holy Cross', *Carrow Works Magazine,* XIX (1925), pp. 1–13; 'J. & J. Colman Ltd. Early days at Carrow up to 1874', *Carrow Works Magazine*, XIX (1926), pp. 93–100.1500 in 1874.

2 The cartel in oregrounds iron

Trading relationships in the raw material for steel

Peter King

Many years ago, E. F. Heckscher argued that Sweden held and exploited a monopoly position as the main supplier of iron traded internationally in northern Europe.[1] Subsequent research has modified that view considerably. In particular, the importance of Russian iron in the mid and late eighteenth century has been recognised.[2] However, there was one variety of iron in which Sweden had an absolute monopoly. This was mostly produced in the province of Uppland, which lies north of Stockholm, using ore from the Dannemora mine. The iron was known in England as oregrounds iron and in Sweden as *vallonjärn* [Walloon iron]. It had no rival anywhere.[3] It was mostly exported from the staple port of Stockholm, but arrived there from shipping places in the vicinity of Öregrund, a small port about 70 miles further north.[4] This kind of iron was necessary for the production of the best steel by cementation, and was also used in considerable quantities in naval dockyards. This is indicated by the accounts of steel converters in Sheffield, by the records of the Navy Board, and those of certain importers.[5] The importance of oregrounds iron for steelmakers was established beyond doubt by the late K. C. Barraclough.[6] What neither he nor any one else, at least not in Britain,[7] seems to have recognised is that the supply of this oregrounds iron was the subject of a cartel for a century and a quarter from about 1730. The main object of this article is to describe the cartel and its effects.

I

Before turning to this particular kind of iron, something must be said of iron more generally. Heckscher claimed that the action, taken in Sweden in the middle of the eighteenth century, to prohibit the further expansion of their industry, had the objective of exploiting a monopoly position, by enhancing the price of iron and limiting the supply. Subsequently, this explanation was questioned and others offered. These included preventing

Swedish woods from being over-exploited and the charcoal costs of Swedish ironmasters thus being forced up, as charcoal became scarce.[8] Iron was Sweden's main earner of foreign currency and was accordingly a focus of government policy as far back as the 1620s. For more than a century after that Sweden was by far the most important exporter of iron, but never enjoyed a full monopoly, for most countries also had a native iron industry as well. Sweden's role was generally one of augmenting native production when that failed to satisfy demand. The exceptions to this may be Scotland and Portugal, which seem to have relied heavily on imported iron from the seventeenth century. However, France did not become a significant importer of iron until the 1760s. English imports of Swedish iron were still insignificant in the 1620s, but grew substantially after that. However, from the late 1720s Russia joined Sweden in exporting substantial quantities of iron to England. Indeed, from about that time there was little growth in English imports from Sweden (see Table 2.1).[9] Accordingly, by the time of the Swedish decrees of 1746 and 1753 prohibiting the expansion of production, Sweden had already lost any monopoly that it had previously had. However, there was one kind of iron, oregrounds iron, in which Sweden did have a complete monopoly and that commodity is the main subject of this article.

Table 2.1 Iron Imports and English Iron Production, 1633–1815

Imports from:	Spain	Sweden	South Baltic	Russia	other	Total	Made in England	Total
1633	1298	26	11		3319	3356	17300	20656
1663	863	5301	20		2479	7800	14200	22000
1685	1292	7351	2		1954	9307	12900	22207
1700	2286	13304	119	142	2852	16417	13200	29617
1714	1269	14190	440	17	2506	17153	13300	30453
1750	916	16747	494	7818	1842	26901	18800	45701
1770	722	16338	241	26711	3399	46689	22100	68789
1815		7905		3496	65	11467	123200	134667

Sources: see note 9.

Imports: 1633: A. M. Millard, 'The import trade of London 1600–1640' (Ph.D. thesis, London University, 1956) i, app. p. 9 and iii, Table C; and from Port Books, cf. S.-E. Åström, *From Cloth to Iron* (as note 9), p. 204; 1663 British Library, Add. Mss. 36785 and from Port Books; 1685: from Port Books, cf. S.-E. Åström, *From Cloth to iron*, p. 204; 1697–1780 Customs Ledgers (P.R.O., CUST 3); 1815 Customs Ledgers (P.R.O., CUST 4). The data refers to England and Wales. The sixteenth- and seventeenth-century data is based on figures for all major ports with interpolation. The eighteenth-century import data is averaged over five years. The production data for 1714 and 1750 is based on the list published in P. W. King, 'Early Statistics for the iron industry' *Historical Metallurgy* 30 (1996), pp. 36–7. The others are interpolated using the data in these lists and other sources.

Iron is not a uniform commodity. Different kinds of iron are suitable for different purposes, and each kind had its own price. Tough (or 'tuf ') iron was needed where the metal would be subject to stresses and strains, as with tools and horseshoes, whereas coldshort iron was quite good enough for most kinds of nails, though not horseshoe nails and clench nails.[10] The difference between these depended largely on the purity of the ore, the haematite ores of the Forest of Dean and Furness producing tough iron and the argillaceous ironstones of the coalfields (with a significant phosphorus content) coldshort. There was an intermediate kind, called blend, which was made by mixing two kinds of pig iron.[11] Robert Morgan of Carmarthen achieved a similar effect by mixing Furness and lower quality local ore, while shipping local ore to Sowley in Hampshire in exchange.[12]

Imported iron was similarly classified in the English market. Ordinary Stockholm iron was equivalent to the best English tough or merchant iron. The best variety of Russian, known as Sable Siberia (and later as Old Sable), was nearly as good, but most Russian iron was worth no more (and often rather less) than English coldshort.[13] However, as already noted, oregrounds iron had no rival. It was necessary for making good steel by the cementation process, and was also used in the building and repair of naval ships.

Oregrounds iron was bought for the British Navy in considerable quantities. For example, in March 1756 the Navy Board made its annual contract with Hugh Ross for 1571 tons of iron, of which five-sixths were to be oregrounds and three-sixths best oregrounds.[14] The start of the Navy Board's purchases coincided approximately (though not quite precisely) with its decision (at the request of the Admiralty) to employ the smiths directly, rather than employing a contractor for smiths' work in each dockyard. However, the Board continued to contract with ironmongers (notably the Crowley family) for ready-made ironware, including nails.[15] From 1726, the Board contracted with London merchants for (mainly) Swedish iron. Details of its contracts survive. These not only specified the quantities and prices of iron, but also its types, of which the three most important were first (or best) oregrounds, second oregrounds, and Stockholm. Other kinds purchased were Siberian, Spanish, Gothenburg, and American, but generally in much smaller amounts. The contracts not only specified these grades, but also the 'marks' by which iron of these grades could be identified.[16] These 'marks', as required by Swedish law, were stamped on to each bar at the forge where it was made. Each forge had its own distinctive mark that identified products as its own brand. This was originally a quality control measure, enabling the searchers at the ports of export to identify the source of any bad iron.[17] However, it also enables iron described in accounts and other records by its mark to be identified as from a particular Swedish forge, although it had previously passed through several hands.

The other main users of oregrounds iron were steelmakers using the cementation process (described below). The Crowleys used some Russian 'Sable' iron for this at their works near Newcastle by the 1750s.[18] The use of this brand probably increased over the following century, until in 1841 when 'CCND old sable [was] extensively used in the manufacture of steel'.[19] Otherwise, oregrounds iron was almost invariably used, because this made the best steel. This is again indicated by the marks, recorded by Swedish travellers, in steelmakers' accounts, and in the records of importers who supplied them.[20] By 1750, Sweden certainly had no monopoly in the lower grades of iron. It is possible that Stockholm iron, as the equivalent of the best English, enjoyed a partial monopoly, in that there were only limited supplies of the best English. However, oregrounds iron was unique. Furthermore, first oregrounds, the most sought-after kind, came from just three forges, and second oregrounds from perhaps another dozen. These enjoyed a complete monopoly in their products. The means by which they exploited this position will be examined in due course, but first something more must be said about steel more generally.

II

In recent times, it has been convenient to talk of the iron and steel industry as a single entity, but iron and steel are not the same. Iron may mean cast iron (for example, run from the blast furnace as pig iron) with 4–5% carbon, or wrought iron with none. The distinction became blurred during the twentieth century, because mild steel made by the Bessemer and later processes became cheaper than iron, and so replaced it.[21] The term 'wrought iron' tends to be used by chemists and metallurgists for commercially pure iron, but in customs records (and presumably contemporary commercial usage) it refers to finished ironware, ready for use by consumers. References to 'iron and ironware' and 'ironmongery' seem to be identical with this, but do not include bar iron, which was subject to a lower rate of customs duty.[22] Steel lies between these two. It is now produced by stopping the process of fining pig iron before all the carbon is removed. However effective processes of this kind were only developed by Bessemer and others in the mid to late nineteenth century.[23] Before that, steel was a relatively expensive material and not produced in very great quantities. Its advantage compared to iron is that it is harder, so that tools retain a sharp cutting edge longer. Edged tools, such as scythes, were usually made of iron with just a thin strip of steel welded along the cutting edge, so that it would stay sharp. Alternatively, steel was sandwiched between two pieces of iron. Steel was also necessary for making files (for shaping iron), and springs. On the other hand, steel was not used at all where iron would do. Accordingly, nails (for both shipbuilding and house building), hinges and locks, horseshoes, musket barrels, and such like were made of iron.

Before Bessemer, steel was made in a number of different ways. The cementation process was one of the most important of these, and for many years the only one in use in England,[24] that great producer and exporter of metal goods. The cementation process, used from the early seventeenth to the mid nineteenth century and beyond, consisted in putting carbon back into bar iron. The main raw material for steel was therefore bar iron. This was placed in a chest with charcoal dust within a steel furnace. The chest was sealed and the furnace heated for several days to 1050–1100°C, a temperature below the melting point of iron. This enabled carbon to diffuse into the iron, thus converting it to steel.[25] The resultant 'blister steel' was then sometimes subjected to mechanical processes. These included slitting it and then bundling and forging it, to make it more homogeneous and to alter its shape to meet what was required by cutlers, scythesmiths, and other manufacturers. From the mid eighteenth century, some blister steel was melted in a crucible and cast into a more homogeneous material known as 'crucible steel'.[26]

One of the earliest producers of blister steel in England was Sir Basil Brooke of Madeley in Shropshire (in the English West Midlands), who held a patent originally granted in 1614 to William Ellyott and Matthias Meysey of London. However, Brooke was forced to surrender that patent in 1618, because a clause in it prohibiting the import of steel was considered objectionable, Brooke having failed to satisfy market demand.[27] Many years later Thomas Fuller described him in the account of Gloucestershire in his *Worthies* as 'the great steelmaker in this county'.[28] However, while there is ample evidence that Brooke was one of the farmers (that is tenants) of the King's ironworks in the Forest of Dean from 1615 until about 1618, and again from 1628 to 1633, there is no evidence of his having made steel in Gloucestershire.[29] However, he did have steel works at Coalbrookdale in his own Shropshire manor of Madeley, and probably did so by 1622 when it was stated that Brooke had 'set up divers ironworks and furnaces for making steel in the county of Shropshire'.[30] The only known steelworks of the period in Gloucestershire was at Linton, but that probably existed by the 1590s (before the invention of blister steel) and must be presumed to have made steel by some older, and probably less effective process. That steelworks belonged to the Earls of Shrewsbury until the death of Earl Gilbert in 1616 and (like his ironworks) was probably run by employees rather than tenants. After his death, the steelworks passed to the Earls of Kent, one of whom married one of Earl Gilbert's coheiresses,[31] and may well have been let not long after. This chronology does not fit with that of the patent, and the steelworks at Linton is most unlikely to have been used by Brooke.

Joseph Moxon, writing about 1677, knew of English, Flemish, Swedish, Spanish, and Venice steel. 'The Flemish steel is made in Germany in the county of Stiermark [Steiermark, Austria] and the land of Luyck' [presumably Luik i.e. Liège].[32] This is probably the commodity imported later from Rotterdam as 'long German steel'. Graffin Prankard of Bristol imported three brands of such steel in the 1730s, known respectively as 'heart and club', 'bird and pincers' and '3 flower de lus' [i.e. fleur de lis].[33] This kind of steel was particularly hard and was probably used mainly for a few special purposes, such as making the chisels used to cut files. Moxon had also heard of steel being imported from Danzig, which was called 'Swedish steel'. However, examination of many port books covering all the major English ports has failed to show any substantial import of steel either from the Baltic or from Spain, though considerable quantities of iron came from both places.[34] It is accordingly suggested that 'Spanish steel' was not made in Spain and imported, but was made in England from Spanish iron, just as 'Spanish cloth' (a new drapery) was originally made in England from Spanish wool.[35] Ambrose (later Sir Ambrose) Crowley, the great London ironmonger, in 1712 advised his brother James in Stourbridge in the iron manufacturing district west of Birmingham: 'It is highly necessary that you convert Spanish iron if others do it, but for the sake of your reputation be carefull never to sell Spanish for orgroon, but mark it and keep it separate, that you may know how to dispose of each sort.'[36] It is suggested, by analogy, that steel made at Coalbrookdale in Shropshire by Sir Basil Brooke from iron from the Forest of Dean in Gloucestershire would have been called 'Gloucestershire steel'. If so, both Fuller and Moxon were misled by the terminology.

III

Certainly, by the early eighteenth century virtually all the steel made in England was converted from Swedish oregrounds iron. Its quality was known to steel-makers by the 1680s, when John Heydon was using 'Spanish or Swedish barrs, . . . called bullet iron' at his furnace at Tiled House in Kingswinford (near Stourbridge). As K. C. Barraclough pointed out, this 'bullet iron' was almost certainly 'double bullet iron', so called because it bore the mark 'OO' of Österby ironworks in Sweden.[37] The discovery of the particular suitability of this Swedish iron for conversion to steel probably took place in England sometime in the mid seventeenth century. This 'double bullet iron' was certainly being sold by Steven de Geer of Amsterdam (as owner of Österby) to Jacob David of London in 1676. It may be the 'O' iron referred to in the correspondence of David's predecessor Charles Marescoe from 1668. The distinction in the iron trade between oregrounds iron, Stockholm iron, and Gothenburg iron was evidently well established by 1672.[38] Indeed, the use of some kind of Swedish iron for steelmaking had began at least forty years earlier, when the quality of steel made from it was investigated in London in 1631.[39] The iron mentioned in 1631 may well have been oregrounds iron. There had been a great increase in the quantity of iron passing through the Sound (from the Baltic) about 1615 and again about 1627.[40] These increases came immediately after investments made in the Swedish iron industry by Louis de Geer and other Dutchmen, first at Finspång in 1615 and then at Österby (one of the oregrounds works) in 1626.[41] This appears to correlate with a significant increase in the iron imported to London from northern Europe in the early 1630s.[42] This makes it likely that a considerable part of that consisted of oregrounds iron.

An alternative English name used for certain Swedish iron, 'Danks iron', derives from Danzig (now Gdansk), whence iron came before direct imports from Sweden began.[43] The accounts of Fell & Co. of Sheffield in the early eighteenth century suggest that this was a more general term, perhaps covering both Stockholm and oregrounds iron. 'Danks iron' was also used for their plating trade, where less good varieties were adequate. Iron used for plating included 'crossed hammers', which in 1725 cost them £18 5s. per ton, when the best oregrounds cost £20 10s. and second oregrounds cost £19 or more.[44] The use of imported iron is also suggested by Charles Tooker's choice of Rotherham, rather than Sheffield, as the place to make steel. He was making it there before the English Civil War and complained that he had suffered losses by fire in September 1642 and by plundering soldiers in the following May.[45] Charles Tooker and one Morrossey allegedly obtained a Cromwellian patent for making steel, which was countermanded in 1662, but renewed in 1666.[46] The latter patent was actually in the names of Sir John Kearsby [*recte* Reresby] and Sir Thomas Strickland.[47]

The products of the various Swedish forges were well known by their marks to the users of iron in England, though those consumers were very probably often ignorant of the actual names of the forges. Each make of iron was therefore known by a description of its mark, 'double bullet' for Österby, 'hoop L' for Leufsta, 'steinbuck' for Harg, and so on.[48] However, these marks were occasionally changed, perhaps when the forge changed hands. Thus, Ullfors used the mark 'CDG' at one period, but had changed to 'W and two crowns' by 1767, when various versions of that mark were being used by Strömsberg, Vessland, and Ullfors. This appears from the report of Goodricke, the British ambassador, on his discussions with Mr de Geer concerning the possibility of the British government contracting with him direct.[49]

Each mark had its own reputation with the steelmakers and these reputations varied to some extent from time to time. The highest grade, known as first oregrounds came from just three forges, Åkerby, Leufsta (now Lövsta), and Österby. Gimo seems to have gained in reputation by the early nineteenth century, while Åkerby's mark, 'PL crown' lost either its reputation or its identity.[50] The second rank comprised another dozen or so forges, including Forsmark, Gimo, Harg, Vattholma, and Ullfors (see Table 2.2). The details of this classification, along with the lower grade of 'Stockholm iron', are strictly those used by the British Navy Board.[51] Nevertheless, surviving accounts for John Fell's steel trade and for the stock of Walter Oborne, as well as those of the Bristol merchant Graffin Prankard, suggest the Board was merely following the market, not leading it.[52] In buying Swedish iron on contracts for fixed amounts, the Navy Board usually specified the proportions of first oregrounds, second oregrounds, and Stockholm iron.[53] The Navy always expected the best materials to be used for its ships, but one wonders whether first oregrounds iron was really necessary. For example, in 1745 when Hugh Ross advised the Board that he would be unable to supply as much first oregrounds iron as he had contracted to and offered two other marks instead, the dockyard officers reported that the iron of those lesser marks was as good.[54] The judgement of the dockyard staff earlier may also be questioned in that they reported to the Commons in 1737 that certain iron from New England was as good as first oregrounds.[55] Yet neither the Navy Board nor the steelmakers began to use American iron regularly, except that the Navy used some American iron during the Seven Years War.[56]

IV

As K. C. Barraclough showed, neither the quantity of oregrounds iron available, nor that required was very great (see Table 2.2).[57] However, it was a premium product whose supply a relatively small group of people sought to control. In 1763, Gilbert Dixon wrote to David Barclay and Sons of London reporting on a meeting called at Sheffield, to sign a petition for a bounty on the import of American iron, to be financed by a further tariff on Swedish:

> I . . . made the business known to the rulers of the Cutlers Company, who called a meeting of a large number of merchants and manufacturers in this place (those concerned in the Swedish contract and in making English iron only excepted) to consult . . . and every one were averse to the design of imposing . . . duty, being already too hardly saddled with the high price of that commodity already and more particularly orgroone iron (best known for making steel), which is monopolised by a few, who will not part with it but when converted into steel at a very advanced price being now sold £5 per ton higher than it was 20 or 25 years ago.[58]

Table 2.2 Swedish forges making oregrounds iron

Name	Owner	Ironmasters who contract for iron	Licensed output (tons)	Source (output)	
Åkerby	Carl de Geer	Carl de Geer	270	1	
Älfkarleö		M. Hissing	270	1	
Carlholm	C. de Geer	C. de Geer	100	2	
Forsmark	Jennings & Finlay	Jennings & Finlay	430	1	
Gimo	Finlay	Finlay	430	1	
Gysinge	Kinsseusturn		200	2	also Uthon mine
Harg	E. Oxenstierna	Lefebure & Burmaster	450	1	
Harnäs	John Leyell	M. Hissing	105	1	also shipped from Älfkarleby
Iggesund	C. & C. Grill	C. & C. Grill	200	2	also Uthon mine. also shipped from Hellsingel
Leufsta	Carl de Geer	J. Graswer	1400	1	
Öhn	Leyel	M. Hissing	200	2	
Ortala	Nordencrants	Lefebure & Burmaster	120	1	
Österby	Grill	Grill	950	1	
Schebo	A. Nordencrants	Lefebure & Burmaster	420	1	
Söderfors	C. & C. Grill	C. & C. Grill	250	1	
Strömsberg	C. de Geer	C. de Geer	220	1	
Ullfors	C. de Geer	C. de Geer	190	1	
Vattholma		Ceverenits	270	1	shipped from Uppsala
Westland	C. de Geer	C. de Geer	200	2	
Total			6675		

Sources:
1. K. Samuelsson in *Forsmark*, 163.
2. Birmingham Archives Boulton & Watt box 25/6 (discussed in note 48).

Notes: This table is compiled from source 2, save that output figures from source 1 have been substituted where available. The figures in the two sources are generally similar, but source 1 gives several alternative figures for some works, which are considerably lower than those in source 2 and those found elsewhere. For this reason those given in source 2, which only lists certain ironworks have been preferred.

The owner's name for Älfkarleö is blank in source 2, but given in a list of *Platbruk* [plate works] at the end of it.

The third column seems (despite its caption) to contain the merchant house in Stockholm selling the iron.

About 1830, a report to the American Congress indicated that steel made from American iron was sufficient for many purposes, but the best quality blister steel required iron from the Dannemora ironworks in Sweden.

> A house in Hull monopolises all the iron made from Danamora ore, under a contract by which the parties in Sweden are to forfeit £10,000 sterling if they sell to any one else – so that no other European country can furnish a good file, without resorting to England for steel that is made of Danamora iron – this excelling all others in Europe for files and other instruments. The British manufacturers, aware of the advantages of their monopoly continue to extract the same price for their steel delivered in America that they did before the duty on Swedish iron was reduced in England.[59]

The reduction in duty mentioned had been made in 1826, but made little difference to the Stockholm price of ordinary Swedish iron, for which America had replaced Britain as the most important market. However, the makers of oregrounds iron, lacking any competitor, were able to maintain the price of their iron in England. Consequently, the Stockholm price of oregrounds iron rose by the amount of the duty no longer payable, and so also did the producers' profits.[60]

The supply of oregrounds iron was apparently already tightly controlled by 1736. In that year, Richard Dalton, a Sheffield merchant selling imported iron, tried to obtain 7 tons of 'PL crown' (Åkerby) iron, which was enough for a single 'heat', from Richard Blount of London. However, Blount evidently refused to sell him any,[61] perhaps because the importers had agreed not to interfere in each other's markets. In 1749, John Cookson of Newcastle had been buying his oregrounds iron at Hull and asked Hugh Ross of London for his terms. Cookson later wrote to Ross, saying: 'I observe oregrounds iron is under contract to you and two others, but as the prices are higher than what I am at present supplied, I cannot give you an order.'[62] However, in 1751 John Button, another Newcastle steelmaker, was importing iron of some kind direct from Stockholm.[63] The Crowley family's factories at Swalwell, near Newcastle, included steel furnaces. However, the great amounts of iron they consumed, both Swedish and Russian, were usually sent from London largely in the firm's own ships, rather than being imported direct from Sweden and Russia. Their consumption in 1770 amounted to over 2500 tons of bar iron of all kinds.[64]

V

The origins of the cartel are probably to be found at Sheffield, where almost all early eighteenth century references to steelmaking concern just three businesses, owned by Samuel Shore, Thomas (and then his granddaughter Elizabeth) Parkin, and John Fell & Co. As early as 1709, Field Silvester, who made steel for Fell & Co., bought a steel furnace in Beast Market, Rotherham, presumably that formerly owned by Charles Tooker, and Fell & Co. reimbursed him for a quarter of the cost. When that property was next sold in 1717, it had been replaced by a barn.[65] In the 1720s, Fell & Co. paid some rent for Richmond steel furnace. Then in 1737 they contributed to buying it and Darnall Furnace from George Steer, they and Elizabeth Parkin each paying a quarter of the cost and Samuel Shore junior the other half.[66] In neither case do the accounts of Fell & Co. indicate that they received any direct financial benefit from the purchases: they neither used them nor received any payment from any other user.[67] This suggests that these furnaces (like Tooker's) were closed, though Darnall may have been revived later.

The accounts of Fell & Co. record their purchases of oregrounds iron. In the 1720s, they had a number of suppliers, including Richard Sykes (who died in 1726) and Robert Thornton of Hull and Stephen Boughton and Lawrence Victorin of London.[68] However, after 1736 the best marks were only supplied by Richard Sykes (died 1761), and later by his brother Joseph Sykes (died 1805). The latter is also named as a substantial creditor (probably for iron), in the stock book of Walter Oborne, Elizabeth Parkin's heir.[69] In 1761 Joseph Sykes told J. L. Robsahm, a Swedish visitor, that new contracts for the next five years had been concluded with the most important oregrounds stamps, and that the entire production of these would be divided between certain merchants in London, Hull, and Bristol.[70] The dominance of the Sykes importing house continued until the mid nineteenth century, and they are undoubtedly the firm referred to in the report to the American Congress in 1830.[71]

Unfortunately, no detail has been found as to how the cartel was formed. However, around 1730 the English end of the negotiations was apparently being managed by Samuel Shore of Sheffield, rather than by an importer. Graffin Prankard of Bristol was in correspondence with him in 1728 over the purchase of 'PL crown' iron and it appears that Shore visited him in Bristol perhaps once a year. It is possible that Prankard was introduced to this business by John Kettle, the Birmingham steelmaker, whom Prankard described as 'a very good chap [customer] of mine'. Prankard was also in correspondence with Mackey and Craighead in London, and more importantly with Francis (or Frans) Jennings in Stockholm.[72] However, Shore was represented by Worcester (or Worster) & Everard.[73] In 1730, matters were thrown into confusion by the death of the owner of Leufsta and Åkerby, a member of the de Geer family resident in Holland. This apparently led to a new contract being made in spring 1731 with Grill, a Dutch merchant (or perhaps a relative in Stockholm).[74] The following August, Norris & Co. of

London were shipping iron from these forges to Bristol for 'Abram Spooner and Finch'.[75] Entry at the Customs House in Bristol, of Norris' shipments of iron from Stockholm, was made by 'John Parkins for Henry Norris'.[76] The agent John Parkin was the father (though not a close business associate) of Mrs Parkin of Sheffield.[77] Abraham Spooner was at this time probably a leading Birmingham ironmonger, though subsequently also a partner in the Stour ironworks of Edward Knight & Co. His son Isaac Spooner appears in the Bristol port books as an importer of iron in 1789. His colleague, Finch, was probably John Finch, a leading Dudley ironmonger. Neither of them is known to have had steel furnaces and their interest was probably merely as merchants.[78] The commercial relationship between Spooner and Norris was probably not a brief one, as Edward Knight & Co. were in the 1740s buying 'Mullers iron' to slit into rods for nailmaking, and employing Norris as their factor in London.[79] Muller's iron was an inferior variety, made at Olonitz [Olonets] in Russia, but very suitable for nailmaking. In 1733, Graffin Prankard had contracted for that year's production and sold it to slitting mill owners.[80] Prankard continued to deal in oregrounds iron until his bankruptcy in 1740. His principal customers for that were Francis Homfray of Stourbridge and John Kettle of Birmingham, both of whom had cementation furnaces, as did certain other buyers of it.[81]

Swedish archives, quoted by K. G. Hildebrand, similarly throw light on the difficult period in the early 1730s after the death of de Geer, when exporting houses belonging to Grill, Robert Campbell, and Petersen, as well as Francis Jennings, were all bidding for oregrounds iron.[82] From this period of relative chaos Francis Jennings ultimately emerged victorious. His merchant house, which later became John Jennings & Co. and then Jennings and Finlay, was the most important one in Stockholm in the period. It remained such until the firm, which by then owned a number of ironworks, was dissolved in 1761. The partners then divided the business, and their ironworks were gradually sold. Robert Finlay and his new partners remained exporters until they became bankrupt in 1772, by which time the firm had declined into being a rather insignificant merchant house.[83]

The name Finch also occurs in relation to the negotiation of contracts in 1746 in correspondence of the Sykes house in Hull with H. & Pet. Muilman in London and with John Jennings & Co. in Stockholm. The former were asked by Sykes to 'prevail upon him [Finch] to address what iron may come by Hull for our care and what other affairs he may have occasion to transact here'. They suggested Finch's earlier withdrawal of commission business from Richard Sykes had been brought about by 'your neighbour Mr H. Norris and Mr Jennings'. The same letter referred to settling 'M[r] Jennings & Co.'s credit upon your [Muilmans'] house at Amsterdam', as well as to Ross & Co. of London having 'contracted the orgroone iron again'. Sykes declined to increase the quantity or price of what they took.[84] The reference to credit is important because the Swedish ironmasters were dependent on borrowing from their factors in Stockholm (or other ports of export). Security for those advances took in the form of *förlag* (in German, *Verlag*), by which the factors owned the iron produced even before it was made.[85] The English importers were perhaps not in such a strong position. Joseph Sykes in 1761 told J. L. Robsahm, a Swedish visitor, that when Österby had been sold to Mr Grill in 1757, the contract with Mrs de Geer had been cancelled, and he had lost £2000. From this Robsahm concluded that the business was exceedingly profitable to Sykes. It evidently suited the Swedish ironmasters to sell their iron together rather than in competition, because it enabled them to enhance or at least keep up the price. Contracts at a fixed price and lasting several years added security. However, being tied to such a contract in a period of rising Swedish prices could also cause considerable loss, and this was indeed one of the reasons for the sale of Österby in 1757.[86]

VI

There seem to have been a number of the London merchants dealing in oregrounds before 1745. Their identities can be determined from the records of the Navy Board as a major buyer of Swedish iron (including oregrounds). The suppliers included Henry Norris from 1728 to 1731 and Richard Blount in 1737 and 1738. Josias Wordsworth made contracts periodically from 1732 to 1743, including during the period in the late 1730s, when Worster and Wordsworth of Stockholm were the sole recipients of the output of Leufsta and Åkerby. However, his final contract (in 1746) was limited to second oregrounds. Hugh Ross obtained a substantial Navy contract in 1741 and was generally the Board's sole supplier from autumn 1744 until 1758.[87] As indicated by Sykes' correspondence (and also by Swedish sources), the Jennings house were correspondents both of Sykes in Hull and Ross in London, though Richard Blount in London also dealt with Jennings.[88] In 1744, the owners of Leufsta and Österby, both of them members of the de Geer family, were anxious that their iron should be sold together by the same merchant, and a producers' cartel certainly existed from that date.[89] Up to that time, the producers had probably used separate factors, who had respectively sold to Ross and Wordsworth in London, but both of them to Sykes in Hull. For the next 110 years (approximately) only a single firm dealt in first oregrounds iron in each port at any given time.

This represents a shift in the focus of the cartel from the steelmakers of Sheffield to their suppliers. This new focus of the cartel meant that the existing Sheffield steel firms were unable to prevent the erection of several new cementation furnaces in the Sheffield area. These included those erected by Walkers and Booth at Holmes about 1748 and by John Roebuck & Sons at Kimberworth in 1751 (both in Rotherham). There was also one in the village of Darnall (now a suburb of Sheffield) built by the same date, and one in Brelsforth Orchards (later Orchard Place) in Sheffield in 1755.[90] A further steelmaking enterprise of this period was run by the Cutlers Company at Sheffield for the benefit of its members without seeking to make more than a modest profit. Iron for this (some of it second oregrounds) was obtained from Samuel Wordsworth and Joseph Sykes.[91]

The period around 1760 saw turbulence in the market, ending with a change in personnel. Such a high price was being asked for the first sort of oregrounds iron that the Navy Board would not buy any.[92] Jennings and Finlay were succeeded as the greatest Stockholm merchant house by C. & W. Tottie (from 1772 Tottie and Arfwedson) and in London Hugh Ross was replaced by Andrew (or Anders) and Charles Lindegren, who were of Swedish extraction. Over the preceding years, Jennings and Finlay had acquired a number of ironworks, including Forsmark, Gimo, Ortala, and Schebo, all of which produced second oregrounds iron.[93] This conflict of interest may have encouraged the owners of Leufsta and Österby to seek an independent factor. The loss of the contract with them may also have been the cause of John Jennings' withdrawal in 1761 (mentioned above) from his merchant house. Whatever the cause, A. Lindegren & Co. were the Navy's sole supplier from the early 1760s until the early 1780s. After the death of Andrew Lindegren in 1783, his firm became bankrupt and was replaced by John and William Wilson (later John Wilson & Sons).[94] The Wilsons in turn came to grief some twenty-five years later due to the losses of their Scottish ironworks at Wilsonstown. As a result, in August 1808 they had to put all their assets in the hands of trustees for their creditors.[95] Their London importing business was apparently quickly sold, as in early September the Wilsons asked the Navy Board to allow Charles Tottie to complete deliveries on their current contract and to pay Tottie.[96] In effect, probably, that business was sold to Tottie and Arfwedson of Stockholm, who then sent Charles Tottie to London to run it. His firm of Tottie and Compton (later, Tottie, Tabor & Co.)[97] was evidently established so as to be London correspondent of the Stockholm firm.

Though ironmongers' goods bought from contractors might sometimes be made of English iron, the bar iron bought by the Navy for use in its dockyards was mostly Swedish and a considerable part of it was oregrounds. The Navy Board did not buy any British bar iron until 1787, when they bought some from Henry Cort made by his puddling process.[98] However, nothing has been found to indicate that such purchases continued after his bankruptcy in 1789.[99] In 1804, John Knight (Edward Knight's son) and William Taitt each had a contract for 190 tons of iron, which are the first ones for English iron recorded in the Chatham dockyard contracts book. The accounts of John Knight & Co. show sales to 'His Majesty's Navy' for a few hundred tons of iron per year until 1815, but starting with a delivery of 12 tons in 1800.[100] At the end of 1805 the Board determined that half the iron ordered for the following year should be British. At the same time it was also pointed out to them that British iron was delivered within twelve months of the contract, thus making it unnecessary to be looking forward for two and a half years for iron.[101]

In 1807, when there were complaints about the quality of certain second oregrounds, probably from Schebo and Harg, the Navy Board insisted on all its Swedish iron being first oregrounds. This was completely impossible, because the Board wanted more of it than was available. Wilsons offered to make up the difference with their own Scottish iron (evidently from Wilsonstown), and the Board ordered Knight's, Wilsons', and Taitt's iron to be tried against each other. It was reported that the Scottish iron (Wilsons') was as good as the best English iron delivered to the dockyard, but the Board decided to continue contracts with their existing British suppliers.[102] This seems ultimately to have resulted in the Board deciding that the British iron they were receiving was satisfactory, and the whole 1362 tons wanted for 1809 was accordingly ordered from British ironmasters.[103] This was a significant change from 1794 when John Wilson and Son had contracted to supply 1110 tons of oregrounds iron.[104] This provided a considerable cost saving, as the Board was paying £24 per ton for English iron, but more than half as much again for oregrounds.[105] It may be that this, as much as the depressive effects of the Continental System, the British Orders in Council, and American Nonimportation Acts, caused there to be a surplus of oregrounds iron. In 1849, Carl Arfwedson (of Tottie and Arfwedson) recalled 'the great services Sykes did to the Dannemora gentlemen during the six years continuance of the Continental System' when he without objection took the contracted quantity of Dannemora [i.e. oregrounds] iron for which there was little demand.[106]

The decision of the Navy Board in 1809 speaks a great deal about the improved quality of the best British iron following the introduction of Cort's puddling and rolling process.[107] However, it may also be a reflection of the reforms taking place in Naval administration in this period,[108] or of the perceived (or actual) difficulty in importing Swedish iron in wartime. Though both the Navy and the steelmakers had previously required oregrounds iron, their motives for doing so were not identical. The Navy needed its iron to be tough, so that it was capable of standing up to the stresses and strains caused by the sea without breaking. On the other hand, the steelmakers needed iron that would make good steel, that is iron particularly free of impurities, since even quite small amounts of phosphorus prevents good steel being made.[109] The continued (indeed increasing) use of oregrounds iron by steel converters for many years after the Navy stopped buying it clearly indicates that English puddled iron was not yet sufficiently pure to meet their requirements.

Throughout all the changes in London, the Sykes firm in Hull continued its course without interruption. However, as suppliers to the Sheffield steel industry, which was the most important user of oregrounds iron, they were probably in a stronger position than their London contemporaries. The consumption of oregrounds iron evidently increased very greatly in the late eighteenth and early nineteenth centuries. Eventually, the cementation furnaces of Sheffield, and the small number elsewhere in Britain, were apparently consuming virtually all of the oregrounds iron made, leading to the situation (mentioned above) reported to the American Congress in 1830. While the Sykes house probably maintained its control of the first oregrounds iron throughout this period, other firms may still have been able to make contracts for second oregrounds. This applies in particular to the second most important importing house for iron in Hull, which belonged successively to Thomas Mould, Joseph Williamson & Co., and Williamsons and Waller. They were replaced in the early nineteenth century by Wilkinson, Whittaker & Co., who became one of Sykes' successors from the late 1850s.[110] Ultimately, as A. Attman has shown, P. A. Tamm of Österby became dissatisfied with Sykes' refusal to enhance the price further. Contracts were renewed for shorter terms, until in 1855 Tamm broke with the cartel. Carl Arfwedson, whose firm had for so long traded with Sykes, lamented the consequent closure of the 'ancient respectable Sykes house'. During the preceding negotiations he had written of the cartel as 'a useful century old system'.[111] It had generally served all concerned well for a long period, but at last it was no more. This breaking up of the cartel does not seem to have been a consequence of the introduction of new steelmaking technology, though that followed not long after. Bessemer steel was not invented until 1856, and could at first only be made from certain types of pig iron, while puddled steel did not begin to be made in Britain until 1858.[112] The quantity of both blister and crucible steel made in England had increased considerably during the nineteenth century, virtually all of it being made from oregrounds iron. P. A. Tamm was evidently able to get the prices he sought from the merchants who replaced Sykes.

VII

The quantities of steel required by industry were not enormous. As Fell & Co. paid a quarter of the costs of the cartel at Sheffield (see above), it is likely that the 50–60 tons they produced per year in the 1720s was about a quarter of the steel made around Sheffield. Accordingly, total production there may have been 200–250 tons.[113] Graffin Prankard's imports of oregrounds iron through Bristol, for steel furnaces in Birmingham, Stourbridge, and Bristol, amounted to some 200 tons most years in the mid 1730s.[114] However, this probably underestimates production in the Midlands, since 220 tons of Swedish iron was converted at Birmingham in 1737.[115] The Crowleys used about 250 tons at their works near Newcastle in the 1750s.[116] Production at other furnaces in the North and elsewhere in Britain may have been another 100–200 tons,[117] suggesting a total production of about 1000 tons per year. In 1802, about 3000 tons of foreign iron was entering Sheffield, of which about two-thirds was brought by steel firms,[118] while Walkers and Booth of Rotherham perhaps made a further 500 tons of steel. The increase in steel production elsewhere in Britain is harder to gauge, but some expansion had undoubtedly taken place, so that British total steel production could have been perhaps 4500 tons.[119] With the Navy using over 1000 tons and some steel being produced from oregrounds iron in Sweden, the whole of the annual production of oregrounds iron is accounted for (see Table 2.2).[120]

Blister steel made by the cementation process was in the mid 1720s priced at around £25 per ton at Sheffield and a little more at Bristol, but this was barely more than half the price of imported German steel.[121] This meant that Britain had a supply of steel that was relatively both plentiful and cheap. Steel production in Sweden had to be fuelled with either wood or imported coal, neither of which was cheap, though more expensive than bar iron.[122] This provided a competitive advantage to Britain with its abundant cheap coal. Attempts made to introduce English steel technology into France were of limited success, especially when the French patriotically used their own rather than foreign iron. The first successful cementation works in France were not set up until the 1750s, imported English or German steel having previously been used. In this they were not alone. A steel furnace established at Rance in the Austrian Netherlands in the early eighteenth century, using Swedish iron, similarly produced steel of a disastrous quality.[123] The need to use particular varieties of Swedish iron, which had been bought up by others years in advance, was certainly known to some people connected with the business in France. A steel-making concern at Nérouville and Souppes did achieve some success when using Swedish iron, but it is evident that the French were technologically a long way behind the English in developing steel production.[124] Nevertheless, the inability of the French to make steel as well as the English can be attributed, at least in part, to their inability to obtain the best marks of iron. This was the result of the existence of the cartel in oregrounds iron between its Swedish producers and its English importers.

VIII

The impact of the cartel on the iron trade generally was probably modest, because most of it did not use oregrounds iron. In 1750, about 18,800 tons of iron was made in England,[125] compared with 26,900 tons imported. 16,750 tons of this came from Sweden (see Table 2.1), but some 2100 tons of iron were re-exported that year.[126] Accordingly, about 43,600 tons was used in English manufactures, of which oregrounds iron was only a small part. The importers of oregrounds iron also handled other kinds of Swedish and Russian iron,[127] and they might, on occasions, contract for the whole output of an ironworks, as in the case of Muller's iron (mentioned above). However, there is little indication that monopolistic practices prevented free trade in iron of other kinds, whereas the effect of the cartel on supply of oregrounds iron for the production of steel was overwhelming.

In the early seventeenth century, the iron converted to steel was probably from the Forest of Dean. However, by the 1630s the superior qualities of Swedish iron had probably been discovered, and particularly those of iron from certain ironworks in Uppland that used ore from the Dannemora mine. That discovery depended on Swedish iron being imported into England and occurred long before the formation of the cartel. The growth of those imports was in part due to the inability of the English ironmasters to satisfy the demands of manufacturers in the seventeenth century. In this, England differed considerably from France, which did not become a significant importer of Swedish iron until the 1760s.[128]

As mentioned earlier, iron was not a uniform commodity. The best blister steel could only be made from the best oregrounds; other kinds of iron would not do. It was thus possible for a small group to control the market in oregrounds iron completely. As we have seen throughout this chapter, there was a cartel in the early eighteenth century between the Sheffield steel converters, who they bought up and closed rival steel furnaces. However, in the 1730s and 1740s the focus of the cartel shifted to the importers. This was partly due to the erection of new steel furnaces which initially used second oregrounds iron, which was less good but more abundant. At Hull, successive members of the Sykes family appear to have controlled the sale of first oregrounds iron for over 120 years, from the 1730s to the 1850s. Their colleagues in Stockholm were members of the Jennings family until about 1760 and then Tottie and Arfwedson. In London, there was a greater change in personnel and the cartel may only have become firmly established in 1744. However, Hugh Ross was virtually the Navy Board's sole supplier from then until 1758. Subsequently, this role was fulfilled by Andrew (or Anders) Lindegren until the 1780s, and then by members of the Wilson family until 1808, when their importing business was sold to a member of the Swedish Tottie family.

Evidence of the identity of the Bristol party to the cartel is less clear. Graffin Prankard certainly fulfilled this role until he became bankrupt in 1740, when he may have been replaced by Finch and Spooner, who were substantial Midland ironmongers rather than Bristol merchants.

In the late eighteenth century, the technological barriers were overcome to the use of mineral fuel in all stages of iron production. This resulted in a great increase in iron production, with iron being one of the leading sectors in the economy during the Industrial Revolution.[129] Consequently, the need to import iron to satisfy the demands of British manufacturers largely disappeared. However, though the Navy stopped using it in 1809, the need for oregrounds iron to be imported did not cease. It was still needed for conversion into steel, because British iron was insufficiently free of impurities. The existence of a cartel no doubt enabled the Swedish producers to keep the price of this iron high. In turn, this must have increased the price of the files and edged tools made from the steel. However, the effect may have been a modest one, since the steel used was probably a relatively small part of the cost.

In this period before the introduction of cheap Bessemer (and other mild) steel, steel was only used where that was unavoidable. Accordingly, iron was used for nails, horseshoes, and many other things. Iron was also used for the main part of knives, scythes, and other edged tools. However, steel was necessary for springs, files, and the cutting edges of edged tools (whether knives, swords, shears, saws, or scythes). Though the quantity used for edged tools was quite a small part of their weight, their quality depended on that of the steel forming its cutting edge. This in turn depended on the kind of iron used to make that steel. Since the supply of the best iron for that was controlled by the cartel, competitors such as the French could not obtain oregrounds iron. This provided Britain with a competitive advantage in exporting edged tools. This was no doubt a factor in the great growth in the export of 'wrought iron' in the eighteenth century. These exports (excluding nails) rose from barely 1000 tons in 1700 to over 10,000 tons by 1770, and then double that by 1800.[130] That advantage was preserved for Britain by the existence of the cartel. Nevertheless, that advantage was not ultimately due to the cartel, but to the failure of English ironmasters to satisfy the requirements of their customers and to significant amounts of iron being imported from the 1630s. Those imports provided the opportunity for the discovery, perhaps as early as 1630, that the best blister steel was made using oregrounds iron.

Acknowledgements

I am grateful to his Grace the late Duke of Norfolk and for permission to consult the Arundel Castle Muniments (ACM) in Sheffield Archives. The archivists, librarians, and staff of the various libraries and record offices cited in the notes have assisted in finding source material for my research. Professor Malcolm Wanklyn kindly read and commented on an early draft of this chapter.

Notes

1　E. F. Heckscher, 'Un grand chapitre de l'histoire du fer: le monopole Sué-dois' [A great chapter in the history of iron: the Swedish monopoly] *Annales d'Histoire économique et sociale* 4 (Paris, 1932), pp. 127–39, 224–41. This view was critically examined in K. G. Hildebrand, *Fagerstabrukens Historia: sexton och sjuttonhundratalen* [*History of the Fagersta Works: sixteenth and seventeenth century*] (Uppsala 1957), pp. 148–59.

2　K. G. Hildebrand, 'Foreign markets for Swedish iron in the eighteenth century' *Scandinavian Economic History Review* 6 (1958), pp. 3–52; *cf.* N. E. Bang and K. Korst, *Tabeller iver Skibsfart og varetransport gennem Øresund 1497–1660; 1661–1783* [Tables of shipping and goods transport through the Sound] (6 vols. or parts, Copenhagen 1906–1953); Public Record Office [hereafter P.R.O.], Customs Ledgers, CUST 4, *passim.*

3　The two concepts are theoretically different. 'Walloon iron' refers to the process by which it was made, the same finery process that was used in England, whereas 'oregrounds' refers to the port of Örgrund from whose hinterland it mostly came. In practice, they seem to be identical.

4　Anders Floren and Göran Ryden, 'A journey into a market society: A Swedish preindustrial spy in the middle of the eighteenth century' in R. Björk and K. Molin (eds), *Societies Made up of History* (Uppsala, Sweden, 1996), p. 264; K. C. Barraclough 'Swedish iron and Sheffield steel' *History of Technology* 12 (1990), pp. 1–39, especially 7–14. This article was originally published in Swedish in A. Attman *et al., Forsmark & vallonjärnet* [Forsmark and Walloon iron] (Sweden, 1987).

5　The source of the iron is identified by its mark (i.e. brand), as copied into written records (see below). The most important records used for this chapter are the accounts of Fell & Co. of Sheffield for their steel trade from 1710 to 1764. These accounts are included in those of an ironworks business in which there were more partners: Sheffield Archives, Staveley Ironworks Records, SIR/3–11 17–25 [hereafter, when referred to generally, 'Fell accounts']. Also useful is a stock book from the 1760s of Oborne and Gunning (successors to Elizabeth Parkin): Sheffield Archives, Oborne Records, OR/2 [hereafter Oborne Stock Book]. Merchants' papers are exceedingly scarce. However the letter books and accounts of Graffin Prankard, the principal iron importer at Bristol of his day survive: Somerset Record Office, DD/DN/424–42, *passim.* [Record Office is hereafter 'R.O.', and these records are referred to collectively as 'Prankard Records']. The records of the Navy Board are in the Public Office [hereafter 'P.R.O.']. The most useful ones are their contract books, relating to contracts made for fixed quantities of supplies (as opposed to standing contracts): ADM 106/3592–3624; ADM 49/32–3 pp. 120–1. However, these only give brief particulars of each contract. The full text is found in the Portsmouth warrant books, in which warrants (i.e. orders) of the Navy Board to the officers of Portsmouth Dockyard were entered upon their arrival there: National Maritime Museum [hereafter 'N. M. M.'], POR/A/7–21. [These records are hereafter collectively 'Navy Board contract records'].

6 K. C. Barraclough 'Swedish iron and Sheffield steel'.
7 K. G. Hildebrand mentioned joint marketing by two producers from 1744, but did not explore its subsequent development. A. Attman described events in the nineteenth century: K. G. Hildebrand, *Fagersta*, p. 204–8; A. Attman, 'Vallonjärnets avsättning på varldsmarknaden 1800–1914' [The disposal of Walloon iron on the world market 1800–1914] in *Forsmark*, pp. 198–207.
8 K. G. Hildebrand, *Fagersta*, pp. 160–4; *Swedish Iron in the Seventeenth and Eighteenth Centuries: Export Industry before Industrialization* (Jernkontoret, Stockholm, 1992: berghistoriska skriftserie 29), pp. 122–8 164ff.; A. Floren and G. Ryden, 'Journey', pp. 261–3.
9 K. G. Hildebrand, *Fagerstabrukens Historia* i, pp. 8–15, 35–44; K. G. Hildebrand, 'Foreign markets for Swedish iron in the eighteenth century' *Scandinavian Economic History Review* 6 (1958), pp. 3–52; S. E. Åström, *From Cloth to Iron: The Anglo-Baltic Trade in the Late Seventeenth Century: i The Growth, Structure, and Organisation of the Trade* (Societas Scientarum Fennica, Helsingfors 1963: Commentationes Humanarum Littarum 33(1)), pp. 53–5, 204–5 and *passim: cf.* N. E. Bang and K. Korst, *Tabeller*; P.R.O., Customs Ledgers, CUST 4, *passim*; Ivan Lind, *Göteborgs handel och sjöfart 1637–1920: historisk statistisk översikt* [Gothenburg's trade and shipping: an overview of historical statistics] (Göteborg 1923), pp. 26–6. The English production data for 1714 and 1750 are taken from contemporary lists: P. W. King, 'Early statistics for the iron industry: A vindication' *Historical Metallurgy* 30 (1996), pp. 36–7. Seventeenth century import data for other countries and figures on the production of iron in England are taken from my dissertation, 'The Iron Trade 1500–1815: The Charcoal Iron Industry and its Transition to Coke' (submitted for a Ph.D. to the University of Wolverhampton 2003). These are derived from large scale interpolations using data for imports, taken mainly from Port Books (P.R.O., E190, various), and for production, from the lists printed in P. W. King, 'Early statistics' and various ironworks accounts. I hope to publish this material more fully elsewhere. *Cf.* A. M. Millard, 'The import trade of London 1600–1640' (Ph.D. thesis, London University, 1956) i, app. p. 9 and iii, Table C; and British Library, Add. Mss. 36785. Eighteenth century import figures are from P.R.O., Customs ledgers, CUST 3 and averaged over five years. *Cf.* E. B. Schumpeter, *English Overseas Trade Statistics 1697–1808* (Clarendon Press, Oxford 1960). The 1815 import figure is from P.R.O., CUST 4/10.
10 N. M. M., POR/A/1, 22 October 1696.
11 H. R. Schubert, *History of the British Iron and Steel Industry from c. 450 BC to AD 1775* (Routledge and Kegan Paul, London, 1957), pp. 304, 311; B. L. C. Johnson, The Foley Partnerships: The iron industry at the end of the charcoal era' *Economic History Review* 2 ser. 4 (1951–2), pp. 331–5. R. G. Schafer (ed.), *A Selection from the Records of Philip Foley's Stour Valley Iron Works 1668–74*, part i (Worcestershire Historical Society, n.s., 9, 1978), pp. 104–5 and *passim*; *cf. Calendar of State Papers, Domestic 1636–39*, p. 357; *Journal of House of Commons* xxii, pp. 850–4; xxiii, pp. 109–17.
12 National Library of Wales, Griffith E Owen 162, Robert Morgan's Letter Book, 8 December 1759 to 7 June 1760, *passim*.
13 Prankard Records, *passim*. The Sable was the trade mark of Demidov family, who were responsible for the development of the iron industry in the Urals:

54   *Peter King*

A. Kahan, *The Plow, the Hammer and the Knout: An Economic History of Eighteenth Century Russia* (University of Chicago Press 1985), p. 183; for the Demidov family generally see Hugh D. Hudson Jr, *The Rise of the Demidov Family and the Russian Iron Industry in the Eighteenth Century* (Oriental Publishers, Newtonville, Mass. 1986).

14 N. M. M., POR/A8, 19 March 1756.
15 M. W. Flinn, *Men of Iron: The Crowleys in the Early Iron Industry* (Edinburgh University Press, 1962), p. 169 and *passim*. Unfortunately the Board's minutes from this date do not survive and the precise course of events is not quite clear. Two hundred and thirty tons of Swedish iron were purchased in 1723 and then apparently no more until March 1726: P.R.O., ADM 106/3590, pp. 108–10; N. M. M., POR/A/7, 22 July and 3 August 1726.
16 Navy Board contract records, *passim*. The contracts also specified quantities of 'short broads', but this seems to refer to size not origin.
17 Bo Molander, 'Forsmarks stångjärnstämpel in över 250 år' [The bar iron stamp of Forsmark over more than 250 years], *Forsmark*, 71ff.
18 T. and P. Berg (trans.), *R. R. Angerstein's Illustrated Travel Diary 1753–1755* (Science Museum, London, 2001), pp. 258–9; A. Floren and G. Ryden, 'Journey', p. 279.
19 H. Scrivenor, *History*, p. 173.
20 Travellers: Barraclough, *Steelmaking, passim*; steelmakers' accounts: Fell accounts and Oborne Stock Book; merchants: Prankard Records.
21 W. K. V. Gale, *Iron and Steel* (Longmans, London, 1969), pp. 1–9, 55.
22 Book of rates appended to Statute 12 Car. II c. 4 'iron wrought *viz.* Axes, adzes, hoes, armour, bits, knives, locks, fowling pieces, muskets, pistols, scissors, stirrups, all carpenters' and gravers' tools, jackwork, clockwork and all ironmongery ware perfectly manufactured' (spellings modernised). This was rated at 10*s. per cwt.*, whereas bar iron was rated at £7 *per ton* in words; *cf. Oxford English Dictionary* (1989 edn) *s.v.* unwrought 2 'not formed or fashioned by being worked up; still in an . . . unfinished state'; *s.v.* wrought 1c 'shaped, fashioned or finished from rough or crude material'. The context for these definitions is other materials, rather than iron, but is also appropriate to it.
23 R. F. Tylecote, *A History of Metallurgy* (2 edn, Institute of Materials, London, 1992), pp. 164–7; Alan Birch, *The Economic History of the British Iron and Steel Industry 1784–1879* (Frank Cass, London, 1967), pp. 313, 321ff; G. I. H. Lloyd, *The Cutlery Trades: An Historical Essay in the Economics of Smaller Scale Production* (Longmans, London, 1913), pp. 30–63.
24 K. C. Barraclough, *Steelmaking* i, pp. 15–29, 48–53ff.
25 K. C. Barraclough, *Steelmaking* i, pp. 34–5.
26 It must be stressed that the raw material for crucible steel was blister steel: K. C. Barraclough, *Steelmaking before Bessemer: ii Crucible Steel: The Growth of Technology* (The Metals Society, London, 1985), pp. 1–10ff.
27 *Calendar of State Papers, Domestic, 1611–18*, pp. 228, 390; *1619–23*, pp. 18, 57; *Acts of Privy Council 1616–17*, pp. 394–5; *1617–19*, pp. 135, 279, 291, 396; *1619–21*, pp. 2–3, 77; *cf.* P.R.O., Exchequer proceedings, E 112/101/1226.
28 Thomas Fuller, *The History of the Worthies of England* (1662; new edn ed. P. A. Nuttall, New York, 1965) i, p. 547.
29 C. E. Hart, *The Industrial History of the Forest of Dean* (David & Charles, Newton Abbot, 1971), p. 12.

30 P.R.O., Chancery Proceedings, C 2/Jas. I/W2/47. This does not give a precise location, but there were steel works at Coalbrookdale by 1645: M. Wanklyn, 'Early steelmaking at Coalbrookdale' *Shropshire Newsletter* 44 (June 1973), pp. 3–6.

31 The steel works at Linton (on the border of Herefordshire and Gloucestershire) were described as by J. Duncumb as 'established . . . under the auspices of the Duke of Kent' early in the eighteenth century. This seems to be an anachronism for the production of steel in Gloucestershire in 1590 and specifically at Linton by 1608, before the introduction of the cementation process. The steelworks was not mentioned in a lease of (inter alia) Linton Woods in 1630 and may therefore have closed. If so, the references to it found by Duncumb in parish registers, are probably to Steelworks Farm, as it is still known, rather than to an operating steelworks. J. Duncumb, *Collections towards the History and Antiquities of the County of Hereford* (1812) ii(1), pp. 383–4. *Calendar of Shrewsbury and Talbot Manuscripts in Lambeth Palace Library and the College of Arms i Shrewsbury mss. in Lambeth Palace Library* (Historical Manuscripts Commission joint publication 6, 1966), MS. 705, f. 67; MS. 708, f. 66; MS. 708, ff. 174, 209. P.R.O., C 2/Chas. I/K2/58.

32 J. Moxon, *Mechanick Exercises or the Doctrine of Handywork* (1677: 3rd edn, 1703), pp. 57–8.

33 Somerset R.O., DD/DN 424, to Benjohan Furley, 18 December 1728 30(?) April 1729 and 17 January 1731/2.

34 In all over 340 customs port books (P.R.O., class E 190) and customs accounts (P.R.O., E 122) have been examined, primarily with the object of determining the amount of iron imported into England and Wales, but little or no steel was noted as coming from either place.

35 L. Clarkson, *The Pre-Industrial Economy of England 1500–1750* (Batsford, London 1971), pp. 110–11.

36 M. W. Flinn, *Men of Iron: The Crowleys in the Early Iron Industry* (Edinburgh, 1962), p. 28n.

37 Robert Plot, *The Natural History of Staffordshire* (Oxford, 1686), p. 374. K. C. Barraclough, *Steelmaking* i, p. 57.

38 H. Roseveare (ed.), *Markets and Merchants of the Late Seventeenth Century: The Marescoe-David Letters 1668–80* (Oxford University Press for British Academy: Studies in economic and social history, n.s. 12, 1987), nos. 8, 181, 306.

39 *Analytical Index to the . . . Remembrancia . . . of the City of London* (London 1878), p. 528; R. Jenkins, 'Notes on the early history of steel making in England' *Transactions, Newcomen Society* 3 (1922–3), p. 27; K. C. Barrclough, 'Swedish iron', p. 7. The source refers to an investigation under an order of Star Chamber of the quantity of steel to be extracted from Swedish iron. Unfortunately, Star Chamber Records do not survive for this period.

40 N. E. Bang and K. Korst, *Tabeller*.

41 K. G. Hildebrand, *Fagersta*, pp. 40–1, 424–5; M. Nisser, 'Forsmark' in *Forsmark*, pp 34–7.

42 A. M. Millard, 'The import trade of London 1600–40' (Ph.D. thesis, London University, 1956), iii, table C converted to quantities using rates given *ibid.* i, appendix p. 13 from P.R.O., E 190/38/5.

43 H. Zins, *England and the Baltic in the Elizabethan Era* (Manchester University Press, 1972), pp. 232–7.

44 Sheffield Archives, SIR/6, journal for 1725, pp. 24, 63, 68. These journals have a separate pagination for each year, starting at midsummer, and are cited according to the year in which they began. The 'Danks iron' mentioned in these accounts was purchased from James Mowld jun. of Hull. It was identified by its marks (i.e. brands), which are identifiable as those of Swedish forges. This included 'crossed hammers', which was classified as Stockholm iron in Navy Board contracts: N. M. M., Portsmouth Warrant Books, POR/A/19, contract of 21 January 1757, entered at 8 March 1757/8. I have failed to identify which Swedish forge used the 'crossed hammers' mark. English iron was in contrast usually described by the name of the forge from which it came, that is unless it bore more than a generic description such as Forest iron (from the Forest of Dean). Thus in 1629, William Glasbrooke supplied Bringewood iron, Cleobury iron, and Shelsley iron to John Jennens of Birmingham ironmonger: P.R.O., Chancery proceedings, C 2/Chas. I/J5/12.

45 Leeds Archives, Mx/R 1/7. I owe this reference to an unknown referee.

46 K. C. Barraclough, *Steelmaking* i, pp. 74–5; D. Hey, *The Fiery Blades of Hallamshire: Sheffield and Its Neighbourhood 1660–1740* (Leicester University Press, 1991), pp. 185–6. I have failed to find direct evidence of the grant of such a Cromwellian patent. However its lapse is likely actually to have been due to the Restoration, as it would presumably not have been validated by the Act for Confirming Judicial Proceedings 1660 (Statute, 14 Car. II, c. 12).

47 B. Woodcroft, *Titles of Patents Chronologically Arranged* (London, 1854), no. 148; R. Jenkins, 'Notes', p. 24.

48 This stamp, impressed at the forge using a punch, was originally required for quality control purposes, but from the mid eighteenth century was also used to prevent forges exceeding their legal production quota: B. Molander, 'Forsmarks stångjärnstampel', pp. 72–8. As to the names see K. C. Barraclough 'Swedish iron', pp. 1–39; *Steelmaking* i, pp. 173–5; Birmingham Archives, B & W box 25/6. The latter appears to be based on a Swedish stampelbok [stamp book] of the late 1750s. Its date is deduced from the reference in it to Jennings and Finlay as owners of Forsmark, which is correct only from 1755 to 1761, when their partnership was dissolved: M. Nisser, 'Forsmark – ett av vallonbruket kring Dannemora grovor' [Forsmark: one of the Walloon Works around the Dannemora Mine] in *Forsmark*, pp. 54–5. The reference to Nordencrants as owner of Ortala and Schebo [Skebo] probably places it before 1759 when Ortala (and possibly also Skebo) were sold to Jennings and Finlay. The published date of 1756 for the sale of Skebo gives rise to difficulties, which I cannot resolve: Loes Müller, *The Merchant Houses of Stockholm c. 1640–1800: A Comparative Study in Entrepreneurial Behaviour* (Uppsala, 1998: Studia Historica Upsaliensa 188), pp.194–5; K. Samuelsson, *De stora köpmanshusen i Stockholm 1730–1815: en studie i den svenska handelskapitalismens historia* [The great merchant houses in Stockholm 1730–1815: a study in the history of Swedish trade capitalism] (Stockholm, 1951), pp. 109–11.

49 P.R.O., State Papers Swedish, SP 95/115, f. 45. The marks differed from each other only by the number and position of dots forming part of the mark.

50 Compare the names in the 1832 price list quoted by K. C. Barraclough with the marks listed in the accounts of Fell & Co.: K. C. Barraclough, 'Swedish iron', p. 16; Fell accounts, journal entries corresponding to ledger pages entitled 'Danks iron' and 'steel trade'. 'Danks iron' is sometimes included in

'Attercliffe iron', probably because the plating hammer making pans was at Attercliffe Forge.

51 E.g. N. M. M., POR/A/19, 8 March 1757/8.

52 Travellers: Barraclough, *Steelmaking, passim*; and see note 5.

53 Navy Board contract records, *passim*.

54 N. M. M., POR/A/14, 3 January and 19 March 1745/6.

55 *Journal of House of Commons* xxii, pp. 850–1.

56 P.R.O., ADM 106/3606, pp. 1, 78, 128; ADM 49/32, pp. 65, 128, 133, 137. These are the only contracts for American iron listed in the Navy Board contract records.

57 K. C. Barraclough, 'Swedish iron', p. 10; *Steelmaking* i, pp. 173–5.

58 P.R.O., Board of Trade, Trade Papers, CO 323/18/S53.

59 Harry Scrivenor, *A Comprehensive History of the Iron Trade* (1841), p. 398. The appendix with this quotation does not appear in the 1854 edition, which has been the subject of a modern reprint.

60 A. Attman, 'Vallonjärnets avsättning', pp. 192, 194; E. W. Fleisher, 'The beginning of the transatlantic market for Swedish iron' *Scandinavian Economic History Review* 1 (1953), pp. 178–92.

61 John Rylands Library (Manchester), Richard Dalton's letterbook, Bagshawe 5/4/1, 17 September, 29 September, 25 October, 13 November and 10 December 1735.

62 Tyne & Wear Archives, Cookson letterbook, 1512/5571, 2 April and 2 May 1749.

63 P.R.O., Newcastle overseas port book for 1751/3, E 190/252/14. His imports totalled 146 tons in two voyages of the *Betty* and were the only iron imported into Newcastle from Stockholm that year. His furnace was built in 1752 on Old Trunk Staith at Gateshead, adjoining the iron foundry there in which he was also a partner: Gateshead Local Studies Library, Cotesworth Mss, CA/2/116 pp. 149, 153.

64 E.g. P.R.O., Newcastle coastal port book for 1770/1, E 190/269/11. The iron is merely described as 'Russian' or 'Swedish' and it is therefore not possible to distinguish between iron from Stockholm and that from Gothenburg, let alone between oregrounds and other kinds. As to the Crowley family generally see M. W. Flinn, *Men of Iron*.

65 Sheffield Archives, WC/1966; MD/401 and 403; K. C. Barraclough, *Steelmaking* i, pp. 74–5; D. Hey, *Fiery Blades*, pp. 185–6.

66 Sheffield Archives, SIR/8, journal for 1736, pp. 55, 67; journal for 1738, p. 73.

67 The Fell accounts are so detailed that use or payment for use can be ruled out. This is not merely an argument from silence. For Darnall see Barraclough, *Steelmaking* i, pp. 75–7, 85–6; D. Hey, *Fiery Blades*, pp. 188–91; Sheffield Archives, ACM/S99 and CA/13; and the previous note, also Sheffield Archives, SIR/9, 1749 journal, p. 81. For Richmond see Sheffield Archives, TC/699; SIR/6, 1727/46 journal, p. 18; K. C. Barraclough, *Steelmaking* i, pp. 74–7; D. Hey, *Fiery Blades*, pp. 186–8, cf. 229–30; Wakefield deeds registry, BB/233/317.

68 From 1726 to 1731 William Wilberforce was named as a supplier, but this was probably as executor of Richard Sykes, during the minority of his son: *cf.* will of Richard Sykes (died 1726), Hull University Library, DDSY/110/12.

69 Fell accounts; Oborne Stock Book; as to Sykes pedigree see Hull University Library, Sykes collection, DDSY/110/12 and 18; *Burke's Peerage* s. v. Sykes of Sledmere.

58   *Peter King*

70 K. C. Barraclough, *Steelmaking* i, p. 185 from J. L. Robsahm 'Dagbok over en resa i England' [Diary of a tour in England] (Ms. in Kungliga Bibliotek, Stockholm), f. 12–13.

71 A. Attman, 'Vallonjärnets avsättning', pp. 200–7; H. Scrivenor, *Comprehensive History*, p. 398 (quoted above).

72 Prankard Records, e.g. Somerset R.O., DD/DN/424, 12 January 1728/9, 30 November, *c*. 16 December 1728, 8 January and 15 January 1729; 17 May to 28 June 1731 *passim*.

73 *Ibid.*, 29 July 1732. English and Scottish merchants seem (where necessary) to have adopted spellings of their surnames that resulted in their being pronounced correctly by Swedes who read them. Worster's partner may have been Edward Everard, who was by 1738 engaged in importing iron from Stockholm into Kings Lynn, in partnership with Browne (probably Samuel Browne): P.R.O., E 190/456/3. He was presumably replaced at Stockholm by a member of the Wordsworth family, who is named as Worster's partner below.

74 *Ibid.*, 7 April 1731. For the descent of Leufsta see K. G. Hildebrand, *Fagersta*, pp. 425, 428; for the Grill family see K. Samuelsson, *De stora köpmanshusen*, pp. 25, 41.

75 Somerset R.O., DD/DN/424, 4 August 1731. For the Grill family see L. Müller, *Merchant Houses*, pp. 62–8 and *passim*.

76 As to the Parkin family see D. Hey, *Fiery Blades*, pp. 193–4; B. A. Holderness, 'A Sheffield commercial house in the mid eighteenth century: Oborne and Gunning around 1760' *Business History* 15 (1973), pp. 32–44. Elizabeth Parkins was an unmarried businesswoman despite her style as 'Mrs'.

77 P.R.O., Bristol port book for 1731, E 190/1207/2.

78 P.R.O., Bristol port book for 1789, E 190/1207/2 and E 190/1239/1. As to the Spooner family, see L. Ince, *The Knight Family and the British Iron Industry* (1991), ch. 3. For the pedigree of the Finch family see R. N. and E. S. Finch, *Our Finch Families and Others* (privately, 1993). For both see also M. B. Rowlands, *Masters and Men in the West Midlands Metalware Trades before the Industrial Revolution* (Manchester University Press, 1975), *passim*.

79 Worcs. R.O., 899:310 BA 10477, Stour ironworks accounts, nos. 141–2, pages entitled 'Making iron at all forges' and 'Mullers iron'. Knight & Co. did not buy Swedish iron. Unfortunately, records for Spooner's business as an ironmonger do not survive. The imports of Mullers iron did not continue into the 1750s: *ibid.*, *cf.* A. Floren and G. Ryden, 'Journey', pp. 286–7; *Angerstein's Diary*, pp. 175–6.

80 Prankard letterbook, 9 February, 23 February 1731/2, 28 June, 7 August 1732. Substantial buyers of this and other Russian iron included John Brindley of Hyde Mill in Kinver, Sampson Lloyd and John Machine of Birmingham, and Francis Homfray and Edward Kendall of Stourbridge, all slitting mill owners: Prankard Records, *passim*; For this trade see also C. Evans, O. Jackson, and G. Rydén, 'Baltic iron and the British iron industry in the eighteenth century' *Economic History Review* 55(4) (2002), pp. 652–4. For particular mills *cf. Victoria County History, Staffordshire* xx, p. 146; *Warwickshire* vii, pp. 256, 264; Dudley Archives, DE4/3, Rowley leases, deed of 24 June 1724.

81 Prankard records, *passim*. C. Evans *et al.*, 'Baltic iron', pp. 656–8. For Kettle: K. C. Barraclough, *Steelmaking* i, p. 95. For Homfray see Dudley archives, D/Pit/7/4; N. Perry, *A history of Stourbridge* (Phillimore, Chichester, 2001), p. 129. I am not convinced by the explanation of Evans *et al.* of the seasonality

of the sales of Russian iron. The dearth of sales between February and August is more likely to be related to the closure of the Baltic by ice in the winter, which prevented the import of iron.

82 K. G. Hildebrand, *Fagersta*, pp. 204–5.

83 K. Samuelsson, *De stora köpmanshusen*, pp. 25, 110–11.

84 Hull University Library, Sykes letterbook, DDSY/101/91, 26 October, 26 November 1746.

85 K. G. Hildebrand, *Swedish Iron in the Seventeenth and Eighteenth Centuries: Export Industry before Industrialization* (Jernkontoret, Stockholm, 1992), pp. 157–8.

86 K. C. Barraclough, *Steelmaking* i, p. 185; K. G. Hildebrand, *Fagersta*, pp. 204–6. The cancellation was made possible by the particular terms of the contract.

87 Navy Board contract records, *passim*; K. G. Hildebrand, *Fagersta*, p. 205. The Wordsworth family came from Sheffield, where other members of it were factors in the cutlery trade: D. Hey, *Fiery Blades*, p. 269.

88 Sykes letterbook as note 75; Riksarkivet (Stockholm), Enskilda Samlingar: arkivfragment: arckivbildare: Frans Jennings correspondence.

89 K. G. Hildebrand, *Fagersta*, p. 205.

90 Holmes: John 1951, pp. 2–3; Kimberworth: Wakefield deeds registry, AD/165/219; AD/702/902; Darnall: *ibid.* AE/486/628; AS/507/681: it is possible this was a revival of the furnace acquired by the three steel firms in 1736. Orchard Place: Sheffield Archives, CB/181, no. 137; CB/1633, map 12.

91 K. C. Barraclough, 'An eighteenth century steelmaking enterprise: The Company of Cutlers in Hallamshire 1759–1772' *Bulletin of the Historical Metallurgy Group* 6 (1972), pp. 24–30.

92 There is clear evidence in their records that the Navy Board only contracted for second oregrounds in 1760 and 1761. This was at a considerably lower price than they had paid in preceding years: P.R.O., ADM 106/3605, p. 62; ADM 106/3606, pp. 24, 169; ADM 106/3607, pp. 117, 158; N.M.M., POR/A/19, 14/2/1758; POR/A/21, 16 September 1760 and 26 February 1762. That they actually *refused* to buy first oregrounds iron appears from a letter of Messrs. Muilman, quoted by K. G. Hildebrand: 'Foreign markets', pp. 29–30.

93 K. Samuelsson, *De stora köpmanshusen*, pp. 111, 234. The situation around 1760 may have been slightly more complicated as Carlos and Claes Grill were apparently dealing direct with Henry and Peter Muilman in 1759 and 1760 and with Andrew and Charles Lindegren in 1761 in respect of Österby iron. However the Grill house was probably less active in overseas trade after the death of Claes Grill in 1767: L. Müller, *Merchant Houses*, pp. 66–7 and 127–8.

94 Navy Board contract records, *passim*; N.M.M., Chatham contracts book 1792–1820, CHA/N/1. Andrew Lindegren's will mentions his contract with Tottie and Arfwedson of Stockholm: P.R.O., PROB 11/1108 q. 467 ff. 153v–54; a dividend in the bankruptcy of Andrew and Charles Lindegren was advertised in 1787; *Aris' Birmingham Gazette*, 14 May 1787. R. A. Mott (ed. P. Singer), *Henry Cort: The Great Finer: Creator of Puddled Iron* (The Metals Society, London 1983), pp. 19–21.

95 P. M. Ritchie, 'The romance of Wilsonstown' *West of Scotland Iron and Steel Inst. Journal* 46 (1937–8), pp. 1–7; I. L. Donnachie and J. Butt, 'The Wilsons of Wilsonstown Ironworks (1779–1813): A study in entrepreneurial failure' *Explorations in Entrepreneurial History* ser. I, 4 (1966–7), pp. 150–68.

96 P.R.O., ADM 106/2671, 6 and 10 September 1808.
97 K. Samuelsson, *De stora köpmanshusen*, p. 46.
98 R. A. Mott, *Henry Cort*, pp. 44–5.
99 *Ibid.*, pp. 57–64; P.R.O., ADM 106/3622; N.M.M., CHA/N/1.
100 N.M.M., CHA/N/1; P.R.O., Navy Board Records, ADM 106/3621, pp. 5, 61–2; Worcs. R.O., 899:310 BA 10470/4, nos. 189–205, particularly no. 189, p. 9; N.M.M., CHA/N/1, 119ff; P.R.O., ADM 106/2668, 26 February 1804. The course of events is not wholly clear because few of the Navy Board's contract books survive for this period. I have only traced a couple of contracts for British iron in the late 1780s, which were for iron made by Henry Cort by puddling: R. A. Mott, *Henry Cort*, pp. 40–6. As to the identities of [John] Knight [of Wolverley, Worcs.] and [William] Taitt [for Dowlais ironworks Merthyr Tydfil] see L. Ince, *Knight Family*, p. 22; L. Ince, *South Wales Iron Industry 1750–1885* (1993), pp. 47–8.
101 P.R.O., ADM 106/2668, 27 December 1805.
102 P.R.O., ADM 106/1655, John Wilson and Sons to Navy Board, 2 and 17 March 1807, 1, 8 and 27 July 1807, and 5 January 1808; ADM 106/2672, 7 March 1809; ADM 106/2673, 15 August 1809; ADM 106/2674, 6 February 1810. For Harg's mark: K. C. Barraclough, *Steelmaking* i, p. 174; for Schebo's mark: B. Molander, 'Forsmarks stångjärnstämpel', p. 83.
103 P.R.O., ADM 106/2672, 31 January 1809.
104 N. M. M., POR/A/37, 29 March 1794.
105 P.R.O., ADM 106/2670, 17 March 1807; ADM 106/2671, 8 April 1808; ADM 106/2672, 31 January 1809. I have not discovered what price Messrs. Wilson were paid at this time, but Mr Grill offered Swedish iron at £37 10s. per ton in 1808. This presumably refers to Claes Grill (d. 1816), a Swedish merchant settled in London from 1770 and Swedish Consul-General 1777–1815: K. Sammuelsson, *De Stora Köpmanhusen*, p. 46.
106 A. Attman, 'Vallonjärnets avsättning', pp. 205–6 (my translation).
107 'We take it for granted [the kind of iron supplied to the dockyards] is the best you manufacture': ADM 106/2674, 26 January 1810.
108 *Cf.* R. Morris, *The Royal Dockyards during the Revolutionary and Napoleonic Wars* (Leicester University Press, 1983), *passim* especially ch. 7.
109 K. C. Barraclough, *Steelmaking* i, pp. 36–7; K. C. Barraclough, 'Swedish iron', pp. 12–14.
110 A. Attman, 'Vallonjärnets avsättning', pp. 200, 207; Gordon Jackson, *Hull in the Eighteenth Century: A Study in Economic and Social History* (London, 1972), p. 97; P.R.O., various Hull port books, E 190/various.
111 A. Attman, 'Vallonjärnets avsättning', pp. 205–6.
112 R. F. Tylecote, *History*, pp. 164–7; Alan Birch, *Economic History*, pp. 313, 321ff.
113 As to the cartel see above; for steel production see K. C. Barraclough, *Steelmaking* i, pp. 70–2.
114 Prankard Records.
115 K. C. Barraclough, *Steelmaking* i, p. 95. A furnace at Birmingham is mentioned to have belonged to Mr Carlesse, who is not mentioned in the Prankard Records.
116 A. Floren and G. Ryden, 'Journey', p. 279.
117 Steel furnaces whose requirements are not taken account of in the forgoing include those at Old Trunk Staith in Gateshead, and Blackhall Mill and

Derwentcote, both in the Derwent valley southwest of Newcastle: D. Cranstone, *Derwentcote Steel Furnace: An Industrial Monument in County Durham* (Lancaster: Lancaster Imprints 6, 1997); for Old Trunk Staith see note 60. By the 1770s there were also furnaces at Cramond near Edinburgh and Dalnotter near Glasgow: K. C. Barraclough, *Steelmaking* i, pp. 98–9.

118 K. C. Barraclough, *Steelmaking* i, pp. 92–3. The context of this concerns goods to be carried on a proposed canal.
119 These figures are estimated in proportion to those for Sheffield.
120 Sweden made 888 tons of steel in 1817: K. C. Barraclough, *Steelmaking* i, p. 124.
121 K. C. Barraclough, *Steelmaking* i, pp. 71–3, 97; Prankard Records.
122 K. C. Barraclough, *Steelmaking* i, pp. 124–6.
123 A. Floren and G. Ryden, 'Journey', p. 291.
124 J. R. Harris, 'Attempts to transfer English steel techniques to France in the eighteenth century' in S. Marriner (ed.), *Business and Businessmen: Studies in Business, Economic, and Accounting History* (Liverpool University Press, 1978), pp. 206–18; J. R. Harris, *Industrial Espionage and Technology Transfer* (Ashgate, Aldershot, 1998), pp. 205–21.
125 P. W. King, 'Early statistics', p. 37.
126 P.R.O., CUST 3/50.
127 This is shown by Hull Port Books (P.R.O., E 190/various) and by there being a number of exporting merchants in Stockholm: K. Samuelsson, *De stora köpmanshusen, passim* especially pp. 237–8.
128 K. G. Hildebrand, 'Foreign markets', pp. 37–40.
129 C. K. Hyde, *Technological Change and the British Iron Industry 1700–1870* (Princeton University Press, 1976), pp. 76–116.
130 E. B. Schumpeter, *English Overseas Trade Statistics 1697–1808* (Clarendon Press, Oxford, 1960), tables viii and ix. The last figure strictly relates to Great Britain. However relatively little iron was manufactured in Scotland. Separate figures on edged tools and other goods containing steel are not available.

Oregrounds iron
Afterword

Peter King

The republication of my 2003 article provides a useful opportunity to reflect on research in the subsequent decades. The most important new work on the subject is Evans and Rydén's *Baltic Iron in the Atlantic World in the Eighteenth Century*.[1] The most relevant section of this focuses on just seven locations, including Bristol, Leufsta, Stockholm, and Birmingham, and on a narrow period, the 1730s. They did not accept my thesis that there was a cartel,[2] but they do note a 1737 sale from Leufsta to three merchants acting in concert.[3] However, it is possible I overstated my case slightly, in that, among the first oregrounds marks, Österby may not have been included in the buying arrangements until a little later. I nevertheless still believe that in the subsequent period, the market was tightly controlled by a handful of merchants, who may properly be called a cartel.

The other development is new light on seventeenth-century steelmaking, something that does not affect my core theme. Paul Belford has published his thesis on Sir Basil Brooke in which he offers a slightly different view of the origins and transfer of the cementation process, suggesting that Brooke had come across the process while abroad.[4] This appeared too late for me to refer to it in my *Gazetteer*.[5] His previous discovery and excavation of the cementation furnaces at Coalbrookdale in Brooke's manor of Madeley also emphasises Brooke's importance.[6] This tends to confirm that (despite his reputation according to Fuller) he did not make his steel in Gloucestershire.[7] A few further details have been identified of the Sheffield steel industry in the late seventeenth century, where four makers were already cooperating in c.1667 having 'agreed between themselves for managing the mystery of making steel'.[8]

Notes

1 C. Evans & G. Rydén, *Baltic Iron in the Atlantic World in the Eighteenth Century* (Brill, Leiden 2007).

2 C. Evans, pers. comm.
3 Evans & Rydén, *Baltic Iron*, p. 98.
4 P. Belford, *Blood, Faith and Iron: A Dynasty of Catholic Industrialists in Sixteenth-and Seventeenth-century England* (Archaeopress Archaeology, Oxford 2018), pp. 153–9, 165–75, particularly p. 158.
5 P. King, *A Gazetteer of the British Iron Industry 1490–1815* (2 vols, BAR British Series 652, 2020), pp. 294, 298.
6 P. Belford and R. A. Ross, 'English steelmaking in the seventeenth century: Excavation of two cementation furnaces at Coalbrookdale', *Historical Metallurgy*, 41(2) (2007), pp. 105–123.
7 See note 28 of chapter.
8 The National Archives [previously P.R.O.], C6/278/9, discussed briefly in King, *Gazetteer*, p. 165.

3 'Made in Britain'? National trade marks and merchandise marks*

The British experience from the late nineteenth century to the 1920s

David M. Higgins

Anglo-German economic rivalry in the fifty years or so before 1914 has received particular attention from business and economic historians. A wide range of explanations have been advanced to explain how Germany was able to challenge successfully many of the key industrial heights which identified Britain as the workshop of the world. These explanations have focused, *inter alia*, upon entrepreneurship,[1] the provision of education,[2] and the interplay between management structures and corporate development.[3] Although the precise weight to be attached to each of these explanations will remain the subject of controversy, for contemporaries, the *perception* of growing German power was equally as disturbing as its reality.

It has been recognised that the perception and the reality of the German threat to Britain's economic hegemony depended on two factors. The first was growing German competition across a wide range of continental, South American, and imperial markets, and the second was the facility with which German manufacturers were able to penetrate the British domestic market.[4] As far as competition in Britain's traditional export markets was concerned, both Hoffman and Buchheim identify the 1870s and 1880s as the decades in which the first serious British fears about German competition emerged.[5] It has also been recognised that concerns about German expansion varied with the trade cycle and the corresponding volume of exports.[6]

However, it was growing German penetration of the British domestic market which elicited the strongest backlash. It has been estimated that Germany's share of total British imports of 'miscellaneous manufactures' increased from 30 per cent in 1880, to 37 per cent in 1896.[7] This figure conceals the fact that for particular types of product, Germany's share of total British imports was very much higher being, for example, 77 per cent and 54 per cent, respectively, for toys and chinaware.[8] Although nearly half of the increase in Germany's *overall* share of British imports was achieved at the expense of other countries, the public perception was, nonetheless, of an overwhelming and irresistible German onslaught on the British market. This sense of unease was captured and then magnified by E. E. Williams in his celebrated book *Made in Germany*.[9] First published in 1896, the book acted as a clarion call to warn of the ubiquity of 'Made in Germany' in all aspects of daily life. Taking as an example the contents of a typical house, Williams warned:

> Roam the house over and the fateful mark will greet you at every turn, from the piano in the drawing room to the mug on your kitchen dresser . . . Descend to your domestic depths, and you will find the very drain pipes German made. You pick out of the grate the paper wrappings from a book consignment, and they also are 'made in Germany'. You stuff them into the fire and reflect that the poker in your hand was forged in Germany. As you rise from your hearth rug you knock over an ornament on your mantelpiece; picking up the pieces you read, on that bit that formed the base, 'manufactured in Germany'. And you jot your reflections down with a pencil that was made in Germany.[10]

Publication of *Made in Germany* coincided with growing accusations of dumping against Germany and growing political agitation for tariff reform in Britain. These two developments were not, of course, unrelated. Tariff protection in Germany enabled her producers to secure such high prices in their domestic market that production was stimulated and surpluses created. It was alleged this surplus production was exported to Britain where it under-sold the products of British manufacturers.[11] This, and other practices, were generally perceived as unorthodox, unfair, and as far as commercial morality was concerned, very dubious indeed.[12]

But there was also a harder edge to the British response and this found its outlet in the campaign for tariff reform. Recent research has shown that several members of the Tariff Commission identified with Germanophobia.[13] That the invasion of the British market by German products should whip up support for tariff reform is hardly surprising, since Germany was Britain's greatest trading competitor and it was recognised that tariff reform could deal a severe blow to Germany. If a tariff war had developed, it seems that Germany would have ended up worse off because the markets of Britain and her Empire were more valuable to Germany than the German market was to Britain.[14]

Although formation of the Tariff Commission seems an entirely logical response to German competition in the British domestic market, its objectives were always undermined by the deep fissures which existed within it.

Research has shown that the contemporary debates which surrounded the tariff reform question cannot be broken down into a simple choice between free trade and protection.[15] However, there existed an alternative to tariff reform in order to meet the German threat, and this was through changes in trade mark and merchandise mark legislation.

This chapter examines the campaign, instigated by the British Empire Trade Mark Association (hereafter, BETMA), to establish the trade mark 'Made in the British Empire'. The BETMA and its campaign appear to have been overlooked in much of the historiography. This seems surprising because if this trade mark had been brought into existence it might have satisfied simultaneously the concerns of free traders and protectionists. Free traders would have been mollified because this mark would not have required the imposition of duties on foreign made products; the protectionist lobby might have been satisfied because the mark would have provided a simple means of identification by which patriotic consumers could exercise their preferences and buy British products. In effect, it was believed that just as the mark 'Made in Germany' had been an outstanding success for German commerce and manufacturing, so too might 'Made in the British Empire' operate to the advantage of Britain.

This chapter is organised as follows. In section I we indicate the key difference between trade marks and merchandise marks. This distinction is important: use of the term 'Made in Germany' was designed to exploit weaknesses in British *merchandise* mark legislation, but registration of the mark 'Made in the British Empire' relied on *trade mark* legislation.[16] In section II we present the background to the legend 'Made in Germany', focussing particularly on the principles and operation of the Merchandise Marks Act (1887), and the way this had acted as an advertisement for Germany. The principal sources of evidence used in this chapter are contained in two parliamentary reports: the Royal Commission on the Natural Resources, Trade, and Legislation of Certain Portions of His Majesty's Dominions, 1912 (hereafter, DRC),[17] and the Minutes of Evidence given before the Merchandise Marks Committee of 1920 (hereafter, MMC).[18] These reports are the key *official* sources on the subject of a British Empire trade mark. In section III we discuss the membership of these committees and analyse the commercial/industrial background of firms supporting the BETMA. In section IV we outline the principles behind the proposals put forward by the BETMA and indicate the favourable changes in trade mark legislation which occurred during its campaign. Sections V and VI discuss the opposition to the British Empire trade mark. Section V focuses upon opposition from owners of private trade marks, and section VI examines the more general problems underlying the scheme. Conclusions are presented in section VII.

I

The central principle guiding the law as it relates to merchandise marks and trade marks is that the deception of the public by the offer for sale of products as possessing some connection with a particular trader, which they do not in fact possess, is wrong, and the trader has a cause of action against any person who is responsible for the deception. Legislation governing these actions falls into two broad categories. The first concerns actions for passing-off and the second concerns actions against infringement of trade marks. In the former case, the complaint is that the defendant is using means which are calculated to pass-off, or cause to be passed-off, the products as those of the plaintiff, and the means *may or may not* consist of the imitation of a trade mark, for example, imitation of the packaging, colouring, and written descriptions which usually characterise a particular product. In the second case, the complaint is that the defendant has infringed his trade mark by taking it in its entirety, or by taking a substantial portion of it.

In effect, therefore, actions for infringement of a trade mark are a specialised sub-group of actions against passing-off. However, until 1875, the only remedy which could be taken was action against passing-off. This was because rights to exclusive legal property in a trade mark had not been effected. Unfortunately, proving that passing-off had occurred was extremely difficult and expensive.[19] Legislation to facilitate these actions was introduced in 1862, but this had only limited success because exclusive legal property in a trade mark was not possible until 1875. The introduction of the Trade Marks Act (1875)[20] remedied this defect. Effectively, from that date, two separate legal remedies were possible. Where a trade mark *itself* was infringed, action could be taken under the Trade Marks Acts. However, where products were passed-off, actions could be taken under the Merchandise Marks Acts.[21]

Although there is a great deal of overlap between the two actions, the key difference is that registration gives exclusive legal ownership of a particular trade mark. Much of the campaign for trade mark legislation was enacted by firms concerned that infringement had devalued the goodwill they had established in their marks. However, individual firms were not the only victims of infringement. During the nineteenth century, the reputation of particular localities and particular nations was also being seriously affected. In the former case, iron and cutlery products marked 'Sheffield' were especially vulnerable to this practice.[22] In the latter case, it appeared that the very reputation of Great Britain herself was under attack as unscrupulous foreign manufacturers and merchants passed-off foreign products as 'British'. Unfortunately, taking action in these cases was very much more difficult because regional appellations were not protected by trade mark legislation. Actions against passing-off in these cases had to rely upon merchandise marks legislation, with all its attendant difficulties. Indeed, as we demonstrate below, it was precisely these difficulties which were to give rise to the legend 'Made in Germany'.

II

Following the passing of the Merchandise Marks Act (1862), three Select Committees were appointed to investigate the working of the law governing merchandise marks.[23] As the law stood in 1862, the fraudulent marking of merchandise did not extend to false indications of origin. A number of Bills were introduced before the House of Commons between 1886 and 1887, in order to remedy this defect.[24] One of the key clauses of these Bills was that false trade descriptions would apply to 'the place or country in which such goods were made or produced'. The Committee of 1887 recognised that this type of fraudulent marking was becoming more pronounced.[25] Accordingly, the Committee gave its support to the Merchandise Marks Law Consolidation and Amendment Bill, the terms of which were enacted as the Merchandise Marks Act (1887).[26] This Act explicitly recognised that the term 'trade description' should embrace the place or country in which goods were made or produced. For our purposes, it was section 16 of the 1887 Act, which is the most important. This section governed the right of customs officers to prohibit the importation of products. Part one of this section stated that:

> All such goods, and also all goods of foreign manufacture bearing any name or trade mark being or purporting to be the name or trade mark of any manufacturer, dealer or trader in the United Kingdom, unless such name or trade mark is accompanied by a definite indication of the country in which the goods were made or produced, are hereby prohibited to be imported into the United Kingdom.[27]

In other words, if foreign products bore any resemblance to a British trade mark, they could not be imported unless they bore an indication of their origin. Herein lies the foundation of the legend 'Made in Germany'. The most damning indictment against the operation of this Act in the nineteenth century was given in evidence before the Committee of 1897. Perhaps the most important weakness of this particular legislation was that German manufacturers continued to mark their goods 'Made in Germany' even when there was no requirement for them to do so (either because, for example, the products did not contain marks which bore any resemblance to British marks or, as was often the case, they bore no marks at all).[28] The irony emerged, therefore, that whereas the 1887 Act was designed to protect against misrepresentation, it had actually served to advertise foreign manufactures, especially those from Germany.[29] This was all the more ironic because whereas German manufactures had a reputation for being 'billig und schlecht', when the 1887 Act was passed, by the 1890s, they enjoyed an unparalleled reputation.[30] As one witness noted, 'The "Made in Germany", which it was intended should vilify German goods in foreign lands has become a mark of honour for the same in the furthest markets.'[31]

It was recognised that the indirect effect of the 1887 Act had been to give foreign countries generally, and Germany in particular, an enormous advertisement,[32] to the extent that the German manufacturer was in favour of, but the British manufacturer was against, the Act![33] More seriously, it was claimed that the mark 'Made in Germany' had been of very great assistance to German trade with the tropics and British colonies.[34]

Clearly, to the extent that British manufacturing was adversely affected by the operation of the 1887 Act, there was a need to minimise or eradicate its pernicious effects. But what measures would achieve this? The most obvious solution appeared to be to remove the requirement for a definite indication of the country of origin, and replace it with a more general term, such as 'Not British'.

On this matter, the Committee of 1897 recognised the weaknesses inherent in Section 16 of the 1887 Act, and indicated it supported the views given in evidence before it that, instead of the specification of the country of origin, the term 'Made Abroad' should be used.[35] This statement produced a flurry of bills, all of which were designed to amend Section 16 of the 1887 Act, by substituting terms such as 'Foreign', 'Made Abroad', 'Not British', or 'British Empire' in place of the actual country of origin.[36] However, none of these Bills succeeded, despite the fact that minor amendments were made to the 1887 Act.[37] There was a need, therefore, for an alternative strategy.

III

We indicated earlier that two parliamentary reports provide the official evidence upon which this chapter is based. In this section we discuss, briefly, the terms of reference upon which these reports were based, before examining the composition of the committees. Since the BETMA was by far the most important body pressing for the registration of the mark, 'Made in the British Empire', it will be particularly useful to examine the composition of its membership.

The DRC was appointed following the Imperial Conference of 1911. This Commission represented the United Kingdom and the self-governing dominions (Canada, Australia, New Zealand, South Africa, and Newfoundland). Its terms of reference were to enquire into all aspects of the production and distribution of food, raw materials, and natural resources in the self-governing dominions, and to investigate the trading links between these dominions and Britain and the wider world. The DRC was particularly desirous of receiving suggestions by which these trading links could be improved and extended.

Although the meetings under the auspices of the DRC lasted seventeen days between October and November 1912, and the minutes of evidence are rather large (extending over three hundred pages), yet the bulk of evidence pertaining to the BETMA is highly concentrated on four days, from Tuesday 5 November through to Friday 8 November. The commission members which heard this evidence were Sir Edgar Vincent, Sir H. Rider Haggard, Tom Garnett, and William Lorimer, representing Great Britain;[38] George Foster (Canada); Donald Campbell (Australia); John Robert Sinclair (New Zealand); Sir Richard Solomon (South Africa); and Edgar Bowring (Newfoundland).

Unlike the DRC, the MMC was exclusively concerned with the operation of merchandise marks legislation. Its terms of reference were threefold: to consider whether existing merchandise marks legislation should be extended as regards indications of origin, to assess the utility and consequences of national and collective trade marks and, finally, to determine whether further international action was necessary for preventing false marking. The MMC sat for fifteen days between 2 December 1919 and 19 March 1920. The membership of the MMC consisted of Messrs. Behrens, Dickie, Everard, Fountain, Temple-Franks, Hood, Hyde, Evans-Jackson, Kerly, Lennox Lee, Moore, Pratt, Wilson, and Levey. Although none of these had sat on previous merchandise marks committees, some of them could be expected to have considerable knowledge and experience of the operation of existing legislation. Thus, for example, both Fountain and Temple-Franks were employed by the Board of Trade, Kerly was a King's Counsel and a recognised authority on the law governing trade marks, and Evans-Jackson was chairman of the patent and trade marks section of the London Chamber of Commerce.

The idea of a British Empire trade mark appears to have originated in the Glasgow Chamber of Commerce, whose directors also suggested that the campaign for the mark should be undertaken by the British Empire Trade Mark Association, a sub-group of the British Empire League.[39] Three reasons were advanced to justify the mark. Firstly, it would provide a simple and definite means of identifying British products and the particular part of the Empire in which they were produced. In addition, it was believed that use of such a mark, in addition to a private trade mark, would make it more difficult and dangerous for imitation to occur. Finally, it was believed that the existence of such a mark would stimulate the demand for British products.[40]

At least in its initial stages, the BETMA appears to have attracted very wide support within Britain and her Empire. Evidence given before the DRC indicates this support comprised three main sections: support from official representatives of the colonies, representatives of British and Empire chambers of commerce, and representatives of British manufacturing. The first category was the least important in numerical terms, comprising thirteen High Commissioners and Agent-Generals representing Canada, Australia, New Zealand, Tasmania, and South Africa. Over 120 chambers of commerce represented their support for the BETMA, with a roughly equal division between British and Empire.[41] The biggest support for the BETMA was to be found within the British manufacturing sector.[42] Over 440 firms were registered as supporting the BETMA. A representative sample of firms supporting the BETMA can be found in Appendix One. This support, though, was highly concentrated on particular industrial groups: textiles, engineering (including metal fabrication), iron and steel manufacture, chemicals, earthenware and glass, leather and hide manufacture, and armaments/shipbuilding. Within these groups, some of the most famous names in British manufacturing can be identified: Ferranti, Ransome, and William Boulton (engineering); Kayser Ellison, Colville, and Hadfields (iron and steel manufacture); Nobels (explosives); Pilkingtons (glassware); Vickers & Sons and Armstrong Whitworth (armaments and warships).[43]

However, as we indicate in later sections, equally powerful opposition was ranged against the BETMA scheme. This opposition had two elements. On the one hand, there were the concerns of owners of private trade marks, while, on the other hand, more general fears were voiced about the administration of the British Empire mark. Before we proceed to discuss this opposition in sections V and VI, it will be useful to examine the principles underlying the BETMA scheme and to review the favourable changes which had occurred in trade mark legislation.

IV

The response of the BETMA to the legend 'Made in Germany' rested on a simple proposition: 'It is now proposed to substitute a positive for the negative sign and, instead of proclaiming that an article is made elsewhere . . . simply to attract our fellow countrymen by a recognised mark proving that it is British made.'[44] It was claimed that just as the mark 'Made in Germany' had been beneficial for Germany, so the mark 'Made in the British Empire' would be equally advantageous to producers in Britain and her Empire.[45]

The BETMA was concerned with the passing-off of foreign goods as British, it believed that adoption of its proposed trade mark would make this type of passing-off more difficult, and it believed its proposed mark would stimulate global demand for British products.[46] The BETMA recognised that, potentially, there were considerable benefits in appealing to the sympathies of consumers in Britain and the British Empire but that, as matters stood, it was practically impossible for consumers to be certain they were buying genuine British products.[47] Boyd, for example, the originator of the BETMA scheme, stated:

> At the present moment I affirm that British produce is not known as such to the ordinary retail consumer ... I cannot myself believe that the ordinary British producer is ashamed in any way to let the consumer know that his goods are British.[48]

Another advantage claimed for this scheme was that it would have the effect of protecting the preferential treatment given to British products by the colonies. It was noted that as the country of origin was not always traceable, a sizeable proportion of non-British Empire products obtained preferential treatment from the colonies.[49] Finally, it was claimed that the operation of the British Empire mark would be of particular benefit to small firms which either did not have their own recognised trade marks or did not have the resources to protect their marks against infringement abroad.[50]

In the period after the Committee of 1897, two developments occurred which justified some degree of optimism about the success of the BETMA scheme. The first was changes to trade mark legislation which were embodied in the Trade Marks Acts of 1905 and 1919. The second was the evident success of the Irish national trade mark in stimulating demand for Irish products. Each of these is considered in turn.

In order to defend successfully against foreign misuse of British appellations, the BETMA would have to secure registration of the term 'Made in the British Empire', as a trade mark. However, although the later nineteenth and early twentieth centuries witnessed considerable diplomatic moves to protect geographical regions from misuse of their appellations, registration under the appropriate trade mark legislation was still a vital pre-requisite.[51] As far as Britain was concerned, this legislation was provided by the Trade Marks Act (1905).[52] Section 62 of this Act, which deals with 'special trade marks', states:

> Where any association or person undertakes the examination of any goods in respect of origin, material, mode of manufacture, quality, accuracy, or other characteristic, and certifies the result of such examination by mark used upon or in connection with such goods, the Board of Trade may, if they shall judge it to be to the public advantage, permit

such association or person to register such mark as a trade mark in respect of such goods . . . when so registered such trade mark shall be deemed in all respects to be a registered trade mark.[53]

Provided that an association could persuade the Board of Trade that it was to the public advantage that they should examine and certify products as being of British, or British Empire origin, the Board of Trade would allow registration of a suitable trade mark. In this respect, Britain was mirroring the developments in other European countries, where state imposed marks existed for the products of industries important to the national economy. Examples of this were the Royal Swedish marks for butter and pork; the Danish Board of Agriculture mark for exported butter; and the marks imposed by the Netherlands Department of Agriculture on butter and bacon.[54] Of course, as we indicate later, precisely which body should be entrusted with administration of the British Empire mark was still to be resolved.[55] Nonetheless, from a purely legal perspective, a potentially vital change in legislation had been obtained. Following this Act, numerous associations registered trade marks under Section 62, to protect the interests of their particular industry. Examples of this include Swanwick & District Fruit Growers Association, the Lincolnshire Curly Coated Pig Breeders' Association, Oxford Down Sheep Breeders' Association, Harris Tweed Association, and the National Pigeon Association![56]

The second development which seemed portentous was the advantage that Irish producers had been able to secure following registration of the Irish national trade mark under the terms of the 1905 Act. Although Britain had a more diverse industrial base than Ireland during this period, the successful operation of the Irish mark appeared to offer the best model upon which the BETMA could organise its scheme.

The Irish national trade mark was promoted by the Irish Industrial Development Association (IIDA), and registered under Section 62 of the Trade Marks Act (1905). It was the first national mark to be so registered.[57] The stated objectives of the IIDA were to promote Irish trade and commerce, to administer the Irish national trade mark, and to take proceedings against persons throughout the world selling or mis-describing non-Irish goods as Irish.[58] Perhaps the most serious obstacle the IIDA had to overcome was to determine what constituted 'Irish' manufacture. For example, was it desirable and feasible to specify a minimum proportion of indigenous labour costs in the final selling price? Alternatively, should there be a specification of the maximum amount of non-Irish inputs into the cost of raw materials?[59] On this latter point, other issues were raised: could the mark be applied, say, to bicycles, all the components of which were imported into Ireland before being assembled?[60] The IIDA decided that under no circumstances would they grant use of the mark if the cost of Irish labour was less than 50 per cent of the total cost of manufacture.[61] Rigorous checks were to be instigated upon firms which had been granted use of the mark.[62] Finally, firms belonging to the IIDA would pay an annual fee, which would be used to finance prosecutions against infringement of the national mark.[63]

The Irish national trade mark appears to have been very successful in stimulating demand for Irish products.[64] It was stated, for example, that the Irish national trade mark had increased the price of cured herrings in Continental markets and enhanced Ireland's reputation in this industry.[65] But there were other benchmarks by which the success of this mark can be judged. One was that over 700 manufacturers had joined the IIDA.[66] Another benchmark was that even the biggest and most reputable Irish firms, such as Gallaghers (tobacco) and Powers and Jameson (whiskey), which had their own valuable private trademarks, were also using the national mark.[67]

In the intervening years between the DRC in 1912, and the MMC in 1920, a further change in legislation occurred which improved the case of the BETMA. We showed earlier that a number of associations were formed to register standardisation trade marks following the Trade Marks Act (1905). Section 62 of this Act permitted registration provided that an association 'undertakes the *examination* of any goods in respect of origin material, mode of manufacture, quality, accuracy or other such characteristic'.[68] The Trade Marks Act of 1919 removed the requirement for examination, requiring only that an association 'undertakes to *certify*' certain characteristics of the products in question.[69] Effectively, the Trade Marks Act (1919) made it easier for the BETMA to satisfy the legal requirements governing registration of its proposed trade mark.[70]

This change in British trade mark law coincided with the ending of the First World War when there was a heightened prejudice against Germany. To begin with, there was recognition by some producers that the use of compulsory marks of origin could be used to discriminate against German goods.[71] In addition, there was real concern about *future* industrial competition from Germany.[72] Some also argued, implicitly, that compulsory marks of origin, in the conditions of the early 1920s, would protect high-cost British firms from low-cost German manufacturers.[73]

Taken together, changes in the legislation governing trade marks, the success of the IIDA, and the re-emergence of Germanophobia after 1919, all appeared to give the BETMA solid grounds for believing that its proposals would be successful. However, even given the propitious circumstances of the immediate post-War years, the BETMA was unable to secure registration of its mark. In the next section, we examine the formidable opposition to the British Empire mark by owners of highly reputable private trade marks.

V

It is, of course, no coincidence that a degree of tension should exist between the interests of owners of private trade marks and proponents of national marks. After all, the reputation that Britain *as a whole* had obtained for her manufacturing products was due, in no small part, to the reputation of individual manufacturers and this, in turn, was due to the importance they placed upon their own trade marks as a guarantee of quality. Clearly, therefore, any proposal for a national trade mark which might impinge upon the goodwill of private trade marks was to be strenuously resisted. Three sources of concern can be identified. Firstly, there was concern about the damage which might be caused to the goodwill already enshrined in private trade marks. Secondly, there was a belief that the British Empire mark, *in addition* to private marks, would generate confusion among consumers. Finally, fears were articulated that the British Empire mark would tend to become a mark of inferiority, thereby damaging both private trade marks and the general reputation of British manufacturers. Representatives of the Lancashire cotton industry were especially vehement in their opposition to the British Empire mark.

Giving evidence before the MMC, the Comptroller General of Patents, Designs and Trade Marks indicated an important distinction between ordinary trade marks, that is, those used by private traders, and national trade marks. The distinction is that whereas ordinary trade marks carry with them the goodwill of the business, national trade marks were not in the least concerned with goodwill or, indeed, with the proprietorship of the specific products to which they were affixed.[74] This distinction explains why many of Britain's biggest and most reputable manufacturers opposed the British Empire mark. Examples of these firms are shown in Appendix Two. These firms feared that the goodwill and value inherent in their own private trade marks would be undermined if they were obliged to adopt the British Empire mark.[75] These fears were summed up by McDowell, managing director of Lever Brothers, as follows:

> The reputation of our manufactures is largely based upon the goodwill attached to our trade marks, and this goodwill has been built up over many years by careful selection of the raw materials used in the manufacture, by care and skill in the methods of manufacture . . . and by the expenditure of several millions sterling in advertising and making known our products . . . We feel that, just as the strength of a chain is its weakest link, so the presence of a common mark upon all brands of soap would be calculated to weaken the reputation of the better brands of soap.[76]

These concerns did not simply reflect arrogance or one-upmanship on the part of Britain's premier manufacturers; they were based upon a real appreciation of the mechanics by which the British Empire mark could undermine private marks. Two means were identified. Firstly, that the adoption of a national mark would cause confusion among consumers, and, secondly, that national marks would eventually become marks of inferiority.

Arguments against the adoption of the British Empire mark were presented most forcibly by representatives of the Lancashire cotton textile trade. The use of trade marks in this industry was exceptionally high: between 1882 and 1892 'cotton marks' averaged 19 per cent of *all* trade mark registrations in Britain, peaking at 45 per cent in 1883.[77] Some of the biggest merchant houses in this trade owned in excess of 500 trade marks, and the seventeen companies represented by Moreton Riley in his evidence to the DRC owned, between them, 27,000 trade marks.[78]

The principal concern of the cotton textile trade was that the complex (or combination of) trade marks which they used in Eastern markets had become extremely valuable. In addition, the indigenous population of these countries had proved themselves especially adept at detecting even the *slightest* deviation in trade marks. Accordingly, it was argued that the addition of an extra mark would be viewed with great suspicion and would lead to much confusion among local buyers.[79] It was even feared that the addition of a national mark would cause offence.[80]

The concerns of the cotton textile trade, that the British Empire mark would eventually become a badge of inferiority, were reinforced by apprehension in other industries.[81] Prior to the Trade Mark Act of 1919, doubts were also expressed about whether big, reputable manufacturers would even agree to inspection of their products in order to be eligible to use the British Empire mark. Crucially, it was feared that if the most reputable manufacturers did *not* use the British Empire mark, this would have the effect of associating this mark with products of inferior quality.[82] As Appendix Two clearly demonstrates, it is difficult to imagine in this period a more reputable group of firms opposing the British Empire mark. Indeed, the British Trade Mark Owners Association argued that many of the firms which supported the British Empire mark had little, if any, proprietary interest in trade marks.[83]

VI

Opposition by the owners of valuable trade marks was not the only obstacle confronting the BETMA scheme. Extremely serious concerns were expressed about the administration of the mark. In this section, we examine these concerns which included, *inter alia*, the impracticability of defining and policing the maximum proportion of foreign inputs to products which would carry the British Empire mark, the problem that national marks of origin might also come to reflect quality, and how realistic it was to believe that the proposed mark could be adopted on an entirely optional basis. Finally, important questions about whether the mark would effectively deter infringement still remained to be resolved.

To begin with, the question of what, precisely, constituted a British Empire product remained paramount. The key problem was that unless a fairly simple definition could be achieved and *enforced*, the public would have no confidence in the scheme or the mark. Exacerbating matters was the fact that, for purposes of imperial preference, the British colonies recognised products as British made only if at least 25 per cent of the manufacturers' cost had been incurred in Britain.[84]

The BETMA realised that it was practically impossible to have a uniform definition of minimum British content, when Britain had such a diverse range of industries, all of which, to a greater or lesser extent, imported foreign components or raw materials. Initially, it appears that the BETMA proposed that the solution to this problem was to leave the matter to sectional committees who would oversee individual industries.[85] However, by 1920 the BETMA appears to have moved in favour of a requirement that British products needed to have a minimum of 25 per cent of the labour done in the British Empire, in order to conform with the rules governing imperial preference.[86] It was also required that firms using the British Empire mark should make a declaration that they did in fact use a minimum amount of British labour.[87]

However, the BETMA scheme could never be as successful as the Irish national mark, which specified that Irish labour costs had to account for at least 50 per cent of the total cost of manufacture.[88] In addition, it was argued that it was precisely because Ireland was so small, both geographically and in terms of the number and range of its manufactures, that the Irish mark would succeed where the British Empire mark would fail.[89]

These doubts were intensified by related fears concerning the ability of national marks to act both as marks of origin *and* quality. The BETMA placed particular emphasis on the fact that its proposed mark was to be a mark of origin; it was not to signify quality.[90] The reason why so much emphasis was put upon this was that the BETMA was concerned that if its proposed mark did indeed come to signify quality, then it might act to the detriment of British products generally, or diminish the value of private trademarks. The BETMA argued that its mark would provide an indication of origin but that the manufacturers' own mark would signify quality.[91]

However, this optimistic viewpoint was subject to considerable criticism. Clearly, to the extent that it was desirable that consumers should be confident that products bearing the British Empire mark contained a minimum percentage of British labour input, what of the corollary that products bearing this mark should guarantee a minimum quality? It appears to have been the case that some witnesses believed the British Empire mark would signify quality, at least to the extent that consumers regarded British products superior to foreign products.[92] In addition, it was thought that if the British Empire mark was used in conjunction with a private trade mark, the former would in time come to denote quality.[93] But, if the British Empire mark did *not* denote quality, this would make it seriously defective, because one of the key roles of a trade mark is to guarantee quality.[94] From this perspective it was feared that unless the mark was a mark of quality it would be exploited by producers of poor-quality goods.[95] This would have the effect of discrediting the reputation of the Empire's producers generally.[96] Conversely, if the mark *was* a mark of quality, it would be impossible to monitor quality standards.[97] Representatives of the Lancashire textile industry argued that it was private trade marks which would be of crucial importance in helping the trade withstand competition from poor quality Japanese exports.[98] Finally, as if the issues raised by this topic were not complex enough, even the BETMA appears to have altered its position, stating that the mark would not be fixed to poor-quality products. In effect, therefore, the mark *would* indicate a minimum quality.[99]

The BETMA tried to allay these fears by emphasising that use of its proposed mark was to be optional, not compulsory.[100] The BETMA recognised the need to overcome the concerns of the owners of private marks, especially those in the Lancashire textile trade. The BETMA argued that since its proposed mark was principally intended as a mark of *origin*, it was difficult to see how it could interfere with the quality enshrined in private trade marks.[101] As far as the Lancashire textile trade was concerned, the BETMA suggested that, since adoption of its mark was intended to be entirely optional, it was up to each firm in the industry to determine whether adoption of the mark was in its best interests.[102]

But even this apparently reasonable viewpoint was subject to criticism. To begin with, if the mark was sufficiently successful that it came into general use, there would be a general expectation of finding the mark on all British Empire products, with the result that those *not* bearing the mark would be viewed with suspicion.[103] This would damage the interests of high-class manufacturers: if they refused to use the British Empire mark, their products might lose the general goodwill attached to British products. However, if they used the British Empire mark, they would be using insignia which was also used by low-quality producers, and this might undermine the goodwill associated with their private marks.[104] In addition, it was believed that once the British Empire mark came into circulation, its use would become absolutely obligatory because manufacturers did not necessarily know the destination of their products. In the same way that German merchants required their manufacturers to mark their products 'Made in

Germany', in case they were exported to Britain, so too, it was believed, the same need would arise with the British Empire mark. Essentially, therefore, adoption of the British Empire mark was a means to ensure that British products would not be refused entry to foreign markets because the country of origin was not indicated.[105] Finally, perhaps the simplest criticism was the most damaging: if use of the mark was not to be compulsory, how could the BETMA be certain that the mark would be used sufficiently to be of any real use to British manufacturing?[106]

The final reservation concerning administration[107] of the British Empire mark, which had still to be overcome, was the extent to which this mark would, in fact, deter infringement. It was argued that administration of the mark under the auspices of the BETMA would be of particular benefit to small-scale manufacturers, who would find the costs and difficulties of taking action abroad insurmountable.[108] It was also believed that the very existence of the BETMA, together with the deployment of its agents throughout the world, would act as a serious deterrent.[109] Finally, it was argued that use of the mark, in addition to private trade marks, would render fraud much more difficult.[110]

However, as with previous claims, these too, were attacked. One problem was that if foreigners had shown considerable facility for infringing private trade marks it was extremely unlikely they would be deterred from infringing the British Empire mark. Indeed, given the reputation of British manufacturing firms, foreign manufacturers might indirectly be encouraged to imitate the British Empire mark, especially if this mark was perceived to have the official endorsement of the British government.[111] Germany and Japan were especially feared in this respect. It was thought they would imitate the British Empire mark to such an extent that this mark would actually damage rather than promote British industry, because the mark would be applied to an increasing volume of products which were not genuine British Empire products.[112] It was further argued that it was the simplest trade marks which had greatest immunity from infringement. To the extent, therefore, that manufacturers thought it desirable to use the British Empire mark in conjunction with their own trade marks, they were actually encouraging imitation![113] Finally, the view was expressed that it was impossible to register the British Empire mark in many countries, with the consequence that proper legal protection could not be obtained, irrespective of the prohibitive costs of undertaking actions for infringement.[114]

VII

This chapter has examined the official contemporary debates surrounding the formation of the British Empire mark. Despite its obvious intuitive appeal, however, the BETMA scheme was not adopted. This appears all the more surprising when we recall the prominence given to the tariff reform question before 1914, as well as the degree of anti-German feeling which existed in Britain immediately after 1919. What conclusions follow from this discussion?

One conclusion which immediately suggests itself is that, perhaps, proponents of the scheme seriously over-estimated the value of the British Empire mark. Indeed, some witnesses argued that it was price and quality which were of prime concern to consumers, not the origin of the products. It was further pointed out that if quality really was the key factor determining consumer preferences, then it was much better to rely on private marks than the country of origin.[115]

A second conclusion is that the dangers of retaliation had not been given sufficient consideration. After all, if the object of the British Empire mark was to advertise British and British Empire products, why shouldn't other countries, in addition to Germany, make a similar response?[116] Viewed from this perspective, there was a distinct possibility that any short-term advantages gained from the British Empire mark would be outweighed by a plethora of competing national trade marks.

It would be tempting to think that part of the explanation for failure of the scheme is that it brought into stark relief the conflicting objectives of merchants and manufacturers. Such an interpretation has received support from recent research[117] and was also commented upon by contemporary observers. Referring to planned extensions of the 1887 Act, for example, Williams noted that: 'Sheffield sees in the Act a protection against German cutlers; London a blow at her trading interests.'[118] However, as far as the British Empire mark was concerned, this interpretation does not appear to be well founded. While it is true, as we have seen, that particular opposition was generated in the Lancashire textile trade, it is also true that equally powerful opposition was forthcoming by reputable firms in other industries. In other words, as far as the British Empire mark was concerned, a simple dichotomy between the interests of merchants and the interests of manufacturers does not appear well founded. In any case, the MMC gave particular emphasis to the absence of agreement on the BETMA scheme. In its report, the MMC stated that:

> No experience has yet been gained anywhere of the use of a mark at all comparable with a national mark for the United Kingdom or a British Empire mark, from which deductions as to the probable utility and effect of such a national or Empire mark could safely be drawn . . . in the absence of agreement among the bulk of the traders concerned, we see grave objections to the institution of a British national or Empire mark.[119]

Nonetheless, perhaps the most important implication which follows from this discussion is that the supporters of the BETMA scheme were proposing a strategy which was backward- rather than forward- looking. For much of the nineteenth century, when Britain was unrivalled in her industrial power, it *was* true to believe that a British Empire mark would have a certain cachet. However, by the late nineteenth and early twentieth centuries, when Britain's manufacturing supremacy was being overtaken, it became harder to believe that this mark would confer a positive image to consumers. In fact, for some countries, especially the USA, there were reasons to believe that such a mark would be disadvantageous.[120] Clearly, to the extent it was believed that a British Empire mark would exercise a deleterious influence on Britain's reputation, further support is given to the view that private, not collective marks, were the key to success in foreign markets.

Appendix One

Representative sample of firms listed as supporting the BETMA scheme[1]

Textiles (broadly defined to include cotton and woollen yarn and cloth manufacturers)
Thomas Ambler & Sons; William Baines & Sons, Ltd; Joshua Baxter & Son; William Birtwistle; Thomas Burnley & Sons, Ltd; N. Corah & Sons; Nile Spinning & Doubling Co., Ltd; Richardson & Co; John Taylors, Ltd; James Walker & Sons; Winder & McKean.

Engineering (including metal fabrication)
Albion Motor Car Co., Ltd; Balfour, Beatty & Co., Ltd; Hobart, Bird & Co., Ltd; The Birmingham Engineering Co., Ltd; William Boulton Ltd; The British Mannesmann Tube Co., Ltd; Cable Makers Association; Davey & Co.; Ferranti Ltd; Loudon Bros. Ltd; The Machine Tool and Engineering Assoc.; A. Ransome & Co., Ltd; Swindon Motor Engineering Co.

Iron and steel
David Colville & Sons, Ltd; Hadfield's Steel Foundry Co., Ltd; Kayser, Ellison & Co., Ltd; Walter McFarlane & Co.; The Old Park Forge, Ltd; Smith, Patterson & Co., Ltd; Watson, Saville & Co., Ltd.

Chemicals
Carless, Capel & Leonard; William Cooper & Nephews; R. & J. Garroway; Charles Massey & Son, Ltd; John Miller & Co.; Procter, Johnson & Co.

Earthenware and glass manufacturers
Allertons, Ltd; Charles Davidson & Co., Ltd; Pilkington's Tile and Pottery Co., Ltd; Twyfords, Ltd.

Leather and hide
Bevington & Sons; The British Leather Cloth Manufacturing Co., Ltd; Martins-Birmingham, Ltd.

Armaments/explosives/firearms/warships
Armstrong, Whitworth & Co., Ltd; Nobel's Explosives Co., Ltd; Vickers, Ltd; Webley & Scott, Ltd.
Source: DRC, 1912, pp. 337–41.

Appendix Two
Examples of firms opposing the BETMA scheme [1]

Cotton manufacturers and spinners
J. & P. Coats, Ltd*; English Sewing Cotton Co., Ltd*; Horrockses, Crewdson & Co., Ltd*; The Calico Printers Association, Ltd*; Richard Haworth & Co., Ltd*; Rylands & Sons, Ltd*; George & R. Dewhurst, Ltd*; Bleachers Association, Ltd*; Bradford Dyers Association, Ltd*; Forbes, Forbes, Campbell & Co., Ltd; Sir Jacobs Behrens & Sons*; Tootal Broadhurst & Lee, Co., Ltd*; J. T. Smith & J. E. Jones, Ltd; Barlow & Jones, Ltd; Glazebrook, Steel & Co., Ltd; Richard Goodair, Ltd; W. Graham & Co; J. Liepmann & Co.'s Successors; Samuel Turner & Co., Ltd; Middleton, Jones & Co., Ltd; F. Steiner & Co., Ltd; Joshua Hoyle & Sons, Ltd*; W. H. L. Cameron, Ltd.

Armourers and engineers
Birmingham Small Arms Co., Ltd; Perry & Co., Ltd; Tangyes, Ltd.

Brewers, distillers and mineral water manufacturers
Arthur Guinness, Son & Co., Ltd; Bass, Ratcliff & Gretton, Ltd*; John Jameson & Son, Ltd; Schweppes Ltd.

Cocoa and chocolate manufacturers
Cadbury Brother Ltd*; J. S. Fry & Sons, Ltd*; Rowntree & Co., Ltd*.

Soap, candle and chemical manufacturers
Brunner, Mond & Co., Ltd*; Lever Brothers Ltd; Joseph Crosfield & Sons, Ltd*; William Gossage & Sons, Ltd*; Price's Patent Candle Co., Ltd; United Alkali Co., Ltd*; Joseph Watson & Sons Ltd.

Potters
Mintons Ltd; J. Wedgwood & Sons, Ltd; Doulton & Co., Ltd.

Match manufacturers
Bryant & May, Ltd.

Biscuit manufacturers
Huntley & Palmers, Ltd; W. & R. Jacob & Co., Ltd.

Preserved meats and confectionery manufacturers
Abram Lyle & Sons, Ltd; James Keiller & Son, Ltd; C. & E. Morton, Ltd;
Samuel Hanson & Son; Crosse and Blackwell, Ltd.

Hat manufacturers
Christy & Co., Ltd

Emery and blacklead manufacturers
John Oakey & Sons, Ltd.

Pen manufacturers
D. Leonardt & Co.

Notes: 1. This list includes companies only. It does not include chambers
of commerce or their representatives who may also have been opposed to
the scheme.
2. * denotes that these companies also opposed the British Empire trade
mark in evidence given before the DRC (1912).
Sources: DRC, 1912; MMC, 1920, p. 232.

Notes

* I am grateful to the editor and an anonymous referee for particularly useful
  comments. I would also like to thank David Jeremy for supplying me with useful material on trade mark legislation.
1 D. S. Landes, The Unbound Prometheus (Cambridge University Press, 1969);
  P. L. Payne, British Entrepreneurship in the Nineteenth Century (Macmillan,
  1974).
2 R. Locke, The End of Practical Man: Entrepreneurship and Higher Education
  in Germany, France and Britain, 1880–1940 (Jaip, 1984).
3 A. D. Chandler, Scale and Scope: The Dynamics of Industrial Capitalism
  (Belknap Press, 1990).
4 R. J. S. Hoffman, Great Britain and the German Trade Rivalry, 1875–1914
  (Russell & Russell, 1964); C. Buchheim, 'Aspects of XIXth century Anglo-
  German trade rivalry reconsidered', Journal of European Economic History,
  Vol. X, 1981, pp. 273–89.
5 Buchheim, 'Aspects of ', pp. 276–82; Hoffman, Great Britain, p. 114.
6 Hoffman, Great Britain, p. 258.
7 Buchheim, 'Aspects of ', p. 285.

84   *David M. Higgins*

8   *Ibid.*, p. 286.
9   E. E. Williams, *Made in Germany* (Heinemann, 1896).
10 Williams, *Made in Germany*, pp. 10–11.
11 Hoffman, *Great Britain*, pp. 31, 45.
12 *Ibid.*, p. 45.
13 A. Marrison, *British Business and Protection, 1903–1932* (Oxford University Press), p. 69.
14 Hoffman, *Great Britain*, especially pp. 284–92.
15 For a discussion of the conflicting political loyalties behind the tariff reform campaign, see, especially, A. W. Coats, 'Political economy and the tariff reform campaign of 1903', *Journal of Law and Economics*, Vol. 11 (1968), pp. 181–229. Even within industries, opinions were highly divided. A. Marrison, 'Businessmen, industries and tariff reform in Great Britain, 1903–1930', *Business History*, Vol. 25 (1983), pp. 148–78.
16 This point requires some elaboration. In order to facilitate international protection against false marking of origin, registration of the appellation as a trade mark was an important first step. So, for example, to prevent Germany marking her products 'Sheffield' it was necessary that this type of appellation be first registered as a trade mark in Britain. A series of International Conventions for the Protection of Industrial Property – Paris (1883), Brussels (1900), Washington (1911) – had established this procedure. For a further discussion of the international issues involved in the protection of appellations see, for example, S. P. Ladas, *The International Protection of Industrial Property* (Cambridge University Press, 1930); D. M. Higgins, ' "Made in Sheffield": Trade marks, the Cutlers' Company and the defence of "Sheffield" ' in C. Binfield and D. Hey (eds), *Mesters to Masters: A History of the Company of Cutlers in Hallamshire* (Oxford University Press, 1997), pp. 93–9.
17 Royal Commission on the Natural Resources, Trade, and Legislation of Certain Portions of His Majesty's Dominions: Minutes of Evidence, Part II: Natural Resources, Trade and Legislation (1912), Cd. 6517. Hereafter, *Report* (1912).
18 Merchandise Marks Committee: Minutes of Evidence (1920). Hereafter, *Minutes* (1920).
19 D. Higgins and G. Tweedale, 'Asset or liability? Trade marks in the Sheffield cutlery and tool trades', *Business History*, Vol. 37 (3) (1995), pp. 10–11.
20 38 & 39 Vict., Trade Marks Act (1875), c. 91.
21 It should be noted that actions for passing-off had a much longer legal history. See, for example, T. A. Blanco White, *Kerly's Law of Trade Marks and Trade Names* (Sweet and Maxwell, 1966), pp. 1–7.
22 Higgins and Tweedale, 'Asset or liability?' pp. 8–17; Higgins, 'Made in Sheffield' pp. 85–114.
23 *Special Report from the Select Committee on Merchandise Marks Act* (1862) *Amendment Bill* (1887); *Report from the Select Committee on Merchandise Marks Act, 1887* (1890); *Report from the Select Committee on Merchandise Marks* (1897).
24 Bill 291, Bill 194, Bill 142, Bill 179.
25 *Special Report from the Select Committee on Merchandise Marks Act* (1862) *Amendment Bill* (1887), QQ. 7–13.
26 50 & 51 Vict., Merchandise Marks Act (1887), c. 28.
27 *Ibid.*, s. 16 (1).
28 *Report from the Select Committee on Merchandise Marks* (1897), QQ. 796, 800, 980, 2679. Hereafter, *S. C. Report* (1897).
29 *Ibid.*, Q. 798.

30 The term means cheap and nasty. For additional views on this point see, for example, D. Head, *Made in Germany: The Corporate Identity of a Nation* (Hodder & Stoughton, 1992), p. 33.

31 *S. C. Report* (1897), Q. 3434.

32 *Ibid.*, QQ. 128, 763, 1223–4, 1265, 1277, 1229–31, 1331, 3624.

33 *Ibid.*, QQ. 841–2.

34 *Ibid.*, QQ. 1029, 1036–7, 1145, 1152.

35 *Ibid.*, p. 4.

36 Bill 58 (1901), Bill 95 (1899), Bill 69 (1902), Bill 36 (1905), Bill 155 (1907), Bill 33 (1907), Bill 25 (1908), Bill 130 (1908), Bill 33 (1904), Bill 353 (1909), Bill 49 (1910). This latter Bill even made provision that were the term 'Not British' used, it should be interlaced in such a way that the word 'Not' could *not* be placed before it. Bill 215 (1911), Bill 12 (1912), Bill 344 (1912), Bill 10 (1913), Bill 57 (1914).

37 54 Vict., Merchandise Marks Act (1891), c. 15; 1&2 Geo. 5, Merchandise Marks Act (1911), c. 31.

38 It is curious that the members of the DRC representing Britain appear never to have acted as committee members or given evidence in the preceding Select Committees of 1887, 1890, and 1897.

39 There was another association formed at this time to promote a more limited scheme. Representatives of firms belonging to the Register of British Manufacturers, sought registration of the mark, 'Made in Britain'. However, apart from the fact that this mark covered a more limited geographical region than the British Empire mark, many of the problems it confronted were identical to those of the BETMA scheme. In addition, it appears from the minutes that representatives of the Register of British Manufacturers were not as prominent in giving evidence as members of the BETMA. See evidence of Mr Sheldrake, *Report* (1912), QQ. 2874–3037.

40 *Report* (1912), p. 342.

41 The Trade Mark Owners Association, though, was quick to point out that chambers of commerce in the big manufacturing centres, which had originally supported the BETMA scheme, had since withdrawn their support. These includes the chambers in Manchester, Birmingham, Sheffield, Bradford, Derby, Liverpool, Walsall, and Dublin. *Report* (1912), p. 343.

42 Merchants were very under-represented. It appears that less than fifteen or so merchants supported the BETMA. As we show later, the merchanting sector, especially in the Lancashire cotton trade, was to be especially vigorous in its opposition to BETMA.

43 For a full listing of commercial institutions (chambers of commerce) and manufacturing firms supporting the BETMA, see *Report* (1912), pp. 336–41.

44 *Minutes* (1920), Q. 4540.

45 *Report* (1912), QQ. 2228–9, 2217, 2221. A similar view was expressed before the Committee of 1897. *S. C. Report* (1897), QQ. 86–7, 860, 471–?

46 *Report* (1912), QQ. 2874, 2918–9, 2217; *Minutes* (1920), QQ. 4543–5;

47 *Report* (1912), QQ. 2874, 2378; *Minutes* (1920), Q. 4540.

48 *Report* (1912), Q. 2220.

49 *Ibid.*, QQ. 2243–6.

50 *Minutes* (1920), QQ. 4627, 4699, 5063–4.

51 Initially, much concerned with particular regions rather than countries: Paris chalk; Brussels carpets. For a further discussion see, for example, Higgins, 'Made in Sheffield', pp. 93–9.

52 5 Edw. 7. Trade Marks Act (1905), Ch. 15.
53 *Ibid.*, s. 62.
54 *Minutes* (1920), Q. 132.
55 For example, unlike the *state* imposed marks in Sweden, Denmark, and the Netherlands, the BETMA was a private association which intended that it should administer its mark.
56 *Minutes* (1920), Q. 135.
57 The mark was registered in 1906. *Minutes* (1920), QQ. 1152–4, 1178.
58 *Minutes* (1920), Q. 1124.
59 In such cases it was policy that if the manufacturer could obtain any or all of his raw materials from Irish sources he would have to do so before use of the Irish national mark would be permitted on the finished article. *Minutes* (1920), Q. 1155. In cases where all the components were imported because such materials were not produced at all in Ireland, use of the mark would be permitted provided that the article was made-up entirely in Ireland. *Report* (1912), QQ. 2621–4, 2693–2701, 2618–21, 2669–72.
60 In such cases, use of the mark was denied. *Minutes* (1920), Q. 1163.
61 *Ibid.*, QQ. 1155, 1413–27.
62 *Ibid.*, QQ. 1264, 1399–1411, 1309–13, 1316.
63 *Report* (1912), QQ. 2660, 2666.
64 *Ibid.*, QQ. 2456, 2513–16, 2517–20, 2555–8; *Minutes* (1920), QQ. 1173–4.
65 *Minutes* (1920), QQ. 1523–6.
66 *Ibid.*, Q. 1432.
67 *Report* (1912), Q. 2553. This point was especially important. We shall see later that it was opposition to the BETMA proposals by some of the biggest and most reputable firms in England and Scotland which proved most damaging. Without exception, these companies feared that adoption of the British marks would grievously injure the goodwill associated with their own private marks. As far as the Irish mark was concerned it appears that, although intended as an origin mark it had, in fact, become a mark of quality. This may explain why big and reputable Irish firms were willing to use the mark. *Ibid.*, QQ. 2680–1, 1175, 1305, 1452.
68 5 Edw. 7. Ch. 15 Trade Marks Act (1905), s. 62.
69 *Ibid.*
70 *Minutes* (1920), QQ. 4570–2.
71 *Ibid.*, QQ. 927–9, 945–6, 2906, 3502, 3522.
72 *Ibid.*, QQ. 2195, 2121, 4559.
73 *Ibid.*, Q. 2461. Some manufacturers, though, argued that their concerns were not motivated by anti-German prejudice. Whether this was an attempt to give their views more objective credibility remains open to doubt. *Ibid.*, QQ. 3406, 3423. In addition, some manufacturers argued that marking of the country of origin would, in fact, promote the competitiveness of British goods. *Ibid.*, Q. 3487.
74 *Ibid.*, Q. 128.
75 *Report* (1912), Q. 3341; *Minutes* (1920), QQ. 766, 926, 2871, 3270, 4892, 5061, 5296.
76 *Minutes* (1920), Q. 4891.
77 D. M. Higgins and G. Tweedale, 'The trade marks question and the Lancashire cotton textile industry, 1870–1914', *Textile History*, 27 (1996), p. 209.
78 *Ibid.*, p. 213; *Report* (1912), Q. 3433.

79 *Report* (1912), QQ. 2219, 3273, 3292, 3591, 3403, 3408, evidence for J&P Coats, Q. 3573 (c), evidence for George Wilkinson, Q. 3581 (point 4), precis of evidence by Behrens & Son, and George Dewhurst & Co, p. 224; *Minutes* (1920), QQ. 1884–92, 1973–6, 2026, 2046, 5250–1, 5251.

80 *Report* (1912), QQ. 3284–6, 3298.

81 *Ibid.*, QQ. 2420, evidence of Finlayson, p. 195, evidence of Brunner, p. 201, QQ. 3319, 3370–2, 3429, 3400; *Minutes* (1920), QQ. 728, 835, 2871, 2937, 3571, 5240, 5252–3, 5296, 5301, 5313. Interestingly, no such criticisms were made about the Irish national trade mark or the legend 'Made in Germany'. In the former case it was argued that except in rare cases, Irish manufacturers were of first class quality, and that there was very little adulteration of Irish products. *Ibid.*, Q. 2538 (p. 155), QQ. 2680–1, 4925–6. In these circumstances, therefore, there was no conflict between private trade marks representing high quality and the adoption of a national trade mark. In the latter case it was suggested that the legend was used by both high-class and low-class producers but nobody assumed that because this legend was used on products of differing quality that these products were of similar quality. *Ibid.*, QQ. 2262–4.

82 *Report* (1912), QQ. 2219, 2900–7, 2910–11.

83 *Ibid.*, p. 343.

84 *Report* (1912), Q. 2874. Even attempts to set a lower limit, say 10 per cent foreign input into a 'British made' article were fraught with difficulties. For example, a motor car with a new and expensive French engine might not be entitled to a 'British' mark, but a car with a cheaper, inferior engine would be entitled to the 'British' mark, because the reduction in its value would bring the total foreign manufactured ingredients below the 10 per cent limit. *Ibid.*

85 *Ibid.*, Q. 2278

86 *Minutes* (1920), QQ. 4682–92, 4833–4, 4837, 4840, 4857, 4871.

87 *Ibid.*, Q. 4593.

88 *Ibid.*, Q. 1155.

89 *Ibid.*, QQ. 2678–9, 2686, 2689, 2712–13. It was recognised that even a purely national trademark, such as 'English' would not overcome trade jealousies. *Ibid.*, Q. 2688.

90 *Report* (1912), Q. 2217; *Minutes* (1920), QQ. 4824, 4549, 4828.

91 *Report* (1912), Q. 2422; *Minutes* (1920), QQ. 4872–5.

92 *Minutes* (1920), Q. 4936. One witness stated it was inevitable that such a mark would become a sign of quality. *Ibid.*, QQ. 3629–30.

93 *Ibid.*, Q. 4872.

94 *Report* (1912), QQ. 3450, 3452, 3541–2; *Minutes* (1920), QQ. 1883, 4133, 4930, 4958, 5054.

95 *Minutes* (1920), Q. 3742.

96 *Ibid.*, QQ. 2909–11, 2935–7, 2738–9, 4122. In addition, of course, if high-quality producers refused to adopt the national mark this might be taken to indicate that their goods were not produced in the British Empire.

97 *Report* (1912), QQ. 3492–3. Other witnesses were to argue that indication of the country of origin was, *ipso facto*, an indication of quality. *Minutes* (1920), QQ. 2669–70, 2681, 4929–30, 4933–4, 5054. In the case of defence of misuse of the appellation 'Sheffield', it was agreed that there might exist variations in the quality of wares entitled to use of this mark. *Ibid.*, QQ. 3632–7.

98 *Minutes* (1920), QQ. 5207–9.

99 *Ibid.*, QQ. 4769, 4805–7, 4678–9.

100 *Report* (1912), QQ. 2217, 2253, 2391–2, 2333; *Minutes* (1920), QQ. 4554, 4585, 4645, 4801.
101 *Report* (1912), QQ. 2421–2; *Minutes* (1920), QQ. 4872–5.
102 *Report* (1912), Q. 2251.
103 *Minutes* (1920), Q. 837.
104 *Ibid.*, QQ. 836–7, 3450, 3619.
105 *Report* (1912), QQ. 3353, 3358, 3381–8.
106 *Ibid.*, Q. 2253.
107 In addition to problems surrounding administration there was a strong objection to the principle of the scheme: it was thought highly undesirable that a national mark should be administered by a private company. *Minutes* (1926), QQ. 136, 1883, 4667, 4705.
108 *Report* (1912), QQ. 2217, 2232, 2323–4, 2326–9; *Minutes* (1920), QQ. 4627, 4741, 4744.
109 *Report* (1912), QQ. 2230–1.
110 *Minutes* (1920), QQ. 4543, 4545.
111 *Report* (1912), QQ. 2217, 3327–31, 3450; *Minutes* (1920), QQ. 4898, 4942, 3547, 5040–2, 5254, 5296.
112 *Minutes* (1920), QQ. 1022–3, 2347, 2430, 2423, 2373.
113 *Report* (1912), QQ. 3448, 3490; evidence of Riley, p. 210, evidence of Oakes (p. 224 (2)), evidence of Clay (p. 226; QQ. 3401–2); *Minutes* (1920), QQ. 4091, 5254.
114 *Minutes* (1920), QQ. 728, 5296, 5299.
115 *Report* (1912), QQ. 2421, 3341, 3619; *Minutes* (1920), QQ. 1908, 2024–5, 2669–72, 2837.
116 *Minutes* (1920), QQ. 3201, 4136–40.
117 Higgins and Tweedale, 'Asset or liability?', p. 14.
118 Williams, *Made in Germany*, p. 139.
119 Merchandise Marks Committee: Report to the Board of Trade of the Merchandise Marks Committee, Cmd. 760 (1920), s. 26.
120 *Report* (1912), Q. 3358.

Made in Britain

A retrospective analysis

David M. Higgins

It is almost twenty years since the publication of 'Made in Britain'.[1] This article focused on the period between the late 1890s and the early 1920s, when Britain was relegated from its position as the world's leading manufacturer. Contemporaries, such as Ernest Williams, pointed to the ubiquity with which products marked 'Made in Germany' appeared in Britain,[2] while others recognised that if Germany benefitted from 'Made in Germany', there was an opportunity for British manufacturers to obtain comparable advantages by adopting a trade mark indicating British, or British empire provenance.

In Britain, evidence on the merits of a 'British' or 'British Empire' trade mark was given before a Royal Commission in 1912, and a Merchandise Marks Committee in 1920.[3] In broad terms, merchants were wholly opposed to such marks. Some manufacturers favoured them, but others did not, though the marks did receive considerable support from representatives of the Dominions.[4] However, fundamental obstacles remained. For example, was the use of such marks to be optional or mandatory? Could the marks be applied to products manufactured from imported raw materials and/or imported semi-manufactures? Finally, which body – Board of Trade, Customs, or a private trade association – determined the rules governing the application of the mark, and its protection? This last hurdle was particularly daunting: if 'British' or 'British Empire' were registered as certification trade marks, a suitable body had to 'certify' the products. Conversely, if registered as collective trade marks, how to ensure they were not abused by 'free riding'? Given this lack of consensus, the Committee of 1920 was unwilling to endorse a 'British' or 'British Empire' trade mark.

In the UK, between 1926 and 1939, the role of merchandise marks to indicate country of origin was enacted by the Merchandise Marks Act, 1926. However, this legislation did not mandate that domestic products be marked 'British', only that certain imported products be marked 'foreign', or 'Empire', or be accompanied by a definite indication of origin, for example, 'Made in Germany'.[5]

Since the publication of 'Made in', research has explored Made in Britain from new perspectives covering different periods. David Thackeray placed Made in Britain firmly in the context of the 'British World' by exploring how consumers in the UK and the British Empire responded to 'Buy British' and 'Buy Empire' campaigns during the interwar period, and how, after 1945, as the EU became the UK's most important trading partner, appeals to patriotism and empire-buying declined.[6]

Subsequent research by David Clayton and David Higgins explored the viability of 'Buy British' by posing three fundamental and complementary questions: first, did domestic consumers display a latent preference for British products? Second, what did 'British' mean, and, finally, how was British provenance to be signalled?[7]

Clayton and Higgins demonstrated that in the late 1970s the Labour government, recognising the potential merits of a 'Buy British' campaign, commissioned Marplan to survey domestic consumers and their attitude toward British products. Over 80 per cent of respondents preferred products to indicate their country of origin. However, while 50 per cent of respondents always made an effort to buy British, or preferred to buy British, this was almost exactly offset (48 per cent) by respondents who claimed they were indifferent between domestic and foreign products, had no preference for buying British, or preferred not to buy British. Reviewing the evidence as a whole, Marplan and the Labour government concluded that a 'Buy British' campaign was unviable.[8]

In 1979, further studies on consumer attitudes to domestic products were undertaken by the National Consumer Council and the National Union of Townswomen's Guilds. With various caveats, the reports revealed that consumers wished to know a product's country of origin. Sally Oppenheim, the Minister for Consumer Affairs who commissioned these reports, recognised that *both* UK and imported products needed to indicate their country of origin. The pretext for this scheme was consumer protection which negated the need for registration of the trademarks 'British' or 'Made in Britain'. But, how to define a 'British' product? Previous UK legislation stipulated that country of origin was the place in which a product last received a substantial change;[9] this definition was used in The Trade Descriptions (Origin Marking) (Miscellaneous Goods) Order, which became effective on 1 January, 1982. However, within three years, this Order was ruled illegal by the European Court of Justice.[10]

Currently, issues relating to country of origin and 'Made in' have resurfaced in global political debate. This is most clearly evidenced by Brexit and ongoing negotiations about the extent to which the UK needs to abide by EU protocols on trade. However, given the rapid and increasing growth in global trade in intermediate products, and the importance of company brands, this author is left speculating whether, in future, consumers will take any notice of the provenance of manufactured products.

Notes

1 David M. Higgins, ' "Made in Britain"? National trade marks and merchandise marks: the British experience from the late nineteenth century to the 1920s', *Journal of Industrial History*, 5 (2002), pp. 50–70.
2 E.E. Williams, *Made in Germany*. London: Heinemann, 1896.
3 *Royal Commission on the Natural Resources, Trade and Legislation of Certain Portions of His Majesty's Dominions*, PP. XVI.393. London: HMSO,1912; *Report to the Board of Trade of the Merchandize Marks Committee*, PP. XXI.615. London: HMSO, 1920.
4 *Royal Commission on the Natural Resources*, p.336.
5 David M. Higgins, *Brands, Geographical Origin and the Global Economy*. Cambridge: Cambridge University Press, 2018: pp. 124–56.
6 D. Thackeray and Richard Toye, 'What was a British buy? Empire, Europe and the politics of patriotic trade in Britain, c.1945–1963', in D. Thackeray, A. Thompson, and R.Toye, (eds), *Imagining Britain's Economic Future, c.1800–1975*. London: Palgrave Macmillan 2018, pp. 133–57; D. Thackeray, *Forging a British World of Trade*. Oxford: Oxford University Press, 2019.
7 David Clayton and David M. Higgins, ' "Buy British": An analysis of UK attempts to turn a slogan into a government policy in the 1970s and 1980s', *Business History* (forthcoming: https://doi.org/10.1080/00076791.2020.1767599).
8 *Ibid.*
9 Trade Descriptions Act, 1968: s8; s.10, s.36.
10 Clayton and Higgins, "Buy British".

Index

advertising: history of 5, 6, 11; policies and practice 20–23, 25; *see also* marketing of branded packaged consumer goods
American iron 40–42

Baker, George 15, 16
Barraclough, K. C. 33, 40
Bessemer steel 36–37, 48
blister steel 37, 49, 50
branded packaged consumer goods *see* marketing of branded packaged consumer goods
Brexit 90–91
British Empire Trade Mark Association (BETMA): administrative issues 76–79; British manufacturing 67–74; campaign launch 66, 69–70; failure of scheme 79–81; firms in support of 81–82; firms opposing 82–83; legal context 67–69; national vs. private marks 75–76; retrospective analysis 89–90
British industrial history: advertising 6; economic hegemony 64; iron demand 42, 47, 49, 51; marketing of branded packaged consumer goods 5–12; personal capitalism 5; steel industry 33, 34, 42–48; this volume 2–3
British national trade marks *see* British Empire Trade Mark Association (BETMA); Made in Britain trade mark
British Navy, use of oregrounds iron 35, 40, 45, 46–47

Brooke, Sir Basil 37, 38, 62
bullet iron 38
business travellers, nineteenth century 10, 15–18

Cadburys 7, 23
cartels, steel industry: changes over time 44–48; impact on the iron trade 50–51; origins 3, 42–44; production volumes 48–49; recent research 62; suppliers focus 45–46
cast iron 36
cementation process, steel 37, 49, 62
Chandler, A. D. 5
Church, Roy 2–3
Clark, Christine 2–3
Clayton, David 90
Colman, Jeremiah 20
Colmans: advertising policies and practice 20, 25; branded packaged consumer goods 7, 13, 20; business travellers 10; origins of modern marketing 7–8, 23–24
commercial travellers, nineteenth century 10, 15–18
competitive advantage: marketing of branded packaged consumer goods 5–6; overview of this volume 2–4; steel industry 49, 51
consumer goods: attitudes to country of origin 90–91; development of marketing 5–6; *see also* marketing of branded packaged consumer goods

94   *Index*

Reckitt, Isaac 8–15, 19–22, 24
Reckitt, James 10, 11, 14, 15
Reckitts: advertising policies and
practice 20–23, 25; marketing
management, family, and partnership
12–14; marketing strategy, selling,
and salesmen 14–18; origins
of modern marketing 7–8, 23,
24; packaging 18–19; product
development 8–10, 24–25; sales
strategy 10–12, 14–18, 25–26
Russian iron 35

sales: marketing of branded packaged
consumer goods 10–12, 25–26;
nineteenth century salesmen 15–18
Sheffield steel 3, 42–44, 45–46, 50
soap makers, nineteenth century 5, 7
special trade marks 72–73
starch industry 8–10, 19–22
steel industry: blister steel 37, 49,
50; cartels and contracts 42–48,
50–51; cementation process
37, 49, 62; distinction from

iron industry 36–37; historical
developments 36–38; oregrounds
iron use 35–36, 38–42, 50;
production volumes 48–49, 50;
Sheffield steel 3; types and grades of
steel 38–40
Stockholm iron 35, 36, 39, 40
Sweden, role as iron supplier to Britain
33–34, 40, **41**, 47–48, 50
Sykes house, Hull 44–45, 48, 50

tariffs, Britain 65–66
tea-dealers 18–19, 23–24
textile trade 76, 78
Thackeray, David 90
trade marks 3; administrative issues
76–79; British manufacturing 67–74;
in law 67–69; and merchandise
marks 66, 67; national vs. private
75–76; quality guarantee 77–78;
retrospective analysis 89–90
Trade Marks Acts 67, 72, 73

Williams, Ernest 65, 80, 89

9780367024154